Essential

Turkey

by

GERRY CRAWSHAW

Gerry Crawshaw has been writing about Turkey's
holiday delights since first discovering them in the early
1970s, and has since acquired an intimate knowledge of
the country, especially its increasingly popular coastal
resorts.

AA

Produced by AA Publishing

Written by Gerry Crawshaw
Peace and Quiet section
by Paul Sterry

Edited, designed and produced
by AA Publishing. Maps ©
The Automobile Association 1994

Distributed in the United Kingdom
by AA Publishing, Norfolk House,
Priestley Road, Basingstoke,
Hampshire, RG24 9NY.

The contents of this publication are
believed correct at the time of printing.
Nevertheless, the publishers cannot
be held responsible for any errors or
omissions, or for changes in details
given in this guide or for the
consequences of any reliance on the
information provided by the same.
Assessments of attractions, hotels,
restaurants and so forth are based
upon the author's own experience
and, therefore, descriptions given in
this guide necessarily contain an
element of subjective opinion which
may not reflect the publisher's opinion
or dictate a reader's own experience
on another occasion.
**We have tried to ensure accuracy
in this guide, but things do change
and we would be grateful if readers
would advise us of any inaccuracies
they may encounter.**

First published 1990
Revised second edition © The
Automobile Association January 1994
Reprinted August 1994, November
1994 and March 1995

A CIP catalogue record for this book
is available from the British Library.

ISBN 0 7495 0844 2

Published by AA Publishing, a trading
name of Automobile Association
Developments Limited, whose
registered office is United Kingdom
by AA Publishing, Norfolk House,
Priestley Road, Basingstoke,
Hampshire, RG24 9NY.
Registered number 1878835.

Colour separation: Mullis Morgan,
London.

Printed by: Printers Trento, S.R.L.,
Italy.

Cover picture: Blue Mosque, Istanbul

Country Distinguishing Signs

On several maps, international distinguishing signs have been used to
indicate the location of the countries which surround Turkey: Thus:

(AZ) = Azerbaijan	(CY) = Cyprus	(IR) = Iran
(ARM) = Armenia	(GG) = Georgia	(IRQ) = Iraq
(BG) = Bulgaria	(GR) = Greece	(SYR) = Syria

MAPS AND PLANS

This book employs a simple rating system to help choose which places to visit:

 ✓ 'top ten' sights

 ◆◆◆ do not miss
 ◆◆ see if you can
◆ worth seeing if you have time

INTRODUCTION

For many thousands of years Turkey has been one of the principal crossroads of the world: a place where camel caravans trekked from the East towards the city now known as Istanbul, delivering spices and silks for the market-places of the West.

Yet until quite recently this vast country, which spans both Europe and Asia, was virtually unknown as a holiday destination, her 5,000 miles (8,000km) of delightful coastline, picture-postcard fishing ports, crystal-clear seas and staggering scenery all but overlooked by the holiday-going public.

Instead, Turkey has been the preserve of 'travellers' as opposed to holiday-makers: people attracted by her myriad reminders of past civilisations: opulent sultans' palaces, Ottoman mosques, awe-inspiring archaeological sites, troglodyte cave-dwellings and ancient thermal pools. People who were happy to forgo

The inner wall of the old medieval fortress of Alanya still keeps watch over what is probably the most picturesque of all the old fishing towns along the Turkish Mediterranean coast

creature comforts and for whom soaking up the sun on a beach held little or no interest.

But suddenly, practically overnight, Turkey burst upon the holiday scene as a major contender in the sun, sea and sand stakes. Tired of the traditional Mediterranean sunspots, and lured by incessant newspaper, magazine and television reports of Turkey's incredibly low prices, holiday-makers began flocking to the country's coastal regions in ever increasing numbers. Major travel companies have leapt on the bandwagon with package holidays aimed specifically at those who care little for Turkey's rich historical past but for whom the idea of heaven is hours of doing nothing, or at least not very much, on a sun-blessed beach.

Unfortunately, much of the accommodation included in those very low cost holidays was of poor standard. Not surprisingly, things began backfiring for the travel companies, and disenchantment with the quality of Turkish holidays among those weaned on the then superior standards offered by countries such as Spain and Greece caused visitor numbers to fall back, especially from the UK.

Recent years, however, have seen the opening of a huge number of stylish and well-equipped hotels and holiday villages in all the major cities, resorts and holiday regions.

Touristic development continues to proceed at a phenomenal pace, especially along Turkey's Mediterranean and Aegean coasts, with new hotels, holiday villages, self-catering apartments, restaurants, bars, discothèques – even brand new, purpose-built holiday resorts – springing up like mushrooms. Airports, roads and other aspects of infrastructure are all developing and improving too, with the result that Turkey is increasingly able to cope with holiday-makers looking for a 'new' destination, but with the creature comforts to which they have grown accustomed.

Historic Sites

Straddling both Europe and Asia, Turkey has been a popular battleground over the ages, playing host to many great empires from the Bronze Age Hittites, Classical Greece and Rome to the Turkish Ottomans. Myth and legend have become entwined with history and tales abound; not surprising when you consider the cast includes Helen of Troy, Jason and the Argonauts, King Midas, Alexander the Great, Antony and Cleopatra and Ottoman sultans such as Mehmet the Conqueror. The impressive remains of Turkey's remarkable history are to be found throughout the country.

A Brief History

The earliest signs of civilisation in Turkey go back to the 6th millennium BC, and it was here that some of the world's first cities were built. Hittite peoples from what was to become the USSR had settled the coast of Asia Minor (as Turkey was known until recent times) by the 13th century BC, and went on to become the undisputed rulers of the whole Near East. That empire eventually collapsed, and Asia Minor became a patchwork of states and tribes with such names as Phrygians, Scythians, Lydians, Assyrians, Persians and Greeks. In time the Persians became dominant, but the Greeks kept their European strongholds, and, at the near-

The ruins of the once-great city of Pergamon, which flourished during the 2nd century BC, attracts many visitors. Its theatre could hold about 10,000 people

legendary battles of Marathon and Salamis, defeated the Persians. Alexander the Great conquered the key cities of Miletos and Ephesus and captured all the cities of the Persian Empire. The next empire to take Asia Minor for its own was the Roman, with the first troops arriving in 201BC. For 600 years Asia Minor was a pivot of the Roman Empire, and in AD330 Constantine moved his capital from Rome to Byzantium, renamed Constantinople. The Byzantine Empire flourished, reaching a pinnacle under Justinian in the 6th century.

In about AD800 tribespeople (principally the Seljuks) who were eventually to become the Turks of today, began an inexorable westward migration from their homelands in Mongolia, Afghanistan and Turkestan. In 1071 they won a great victory against the Byzantine army in eastern Turkey, and eventually arrived at the walls of Constantinople. Before they could take the capital they themselves were overwhelmed by Moghuls, who divided the area into small provinces, one of which, around Bursa, was ruled by the Ottoman dynasty. The Ottomans rapidly gained in power, until by the beginning of the 14th century, they controlled the whole of western Asia Minor. Constantinople remained a Christian bastion in an area that by now had become almost wholly Muslim until 1402, when it went under siege. When it fell at last the Byzantine Empire was ended and, renamed Istanbul, it became the capital of the Ottoman Empire.

By the 16th century, and particularly under Süleyman the Great, the Ottoman Empire had become one of the world's great powers, but its expanding ambitions eventually brought it into conflict with the principal European states. At the same time internal conflicts weakened the Empire, and by the 19th century it was in decline and being attacked on all sides. It struggled on until 1923 when Mustafa Kemal (Atatürk – 'the father of the Turks') took control of the country.

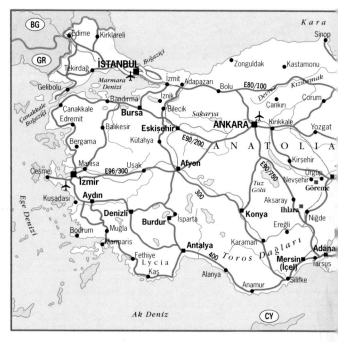

Single-handedly, he wrenched Turkey into the
20th century.
In 1952 Turkey joined NATO, but in the late
1950s the country fell into political trouble which
has continued on and off until now. Under
General Evran, Turkey is once again poised for a
democratic future, and an economic future tied
with the European community.

Special Interest Holidays
Given the variety of Turkey's assets there are
numerous special interest options open to the
holiday-maker looking for more than just a
chance to laze on a beach enjoying the sun with
only an occasional foray to an ancient site.
Watersports are the most popular of these,
including windsurfing, waterskiing, diving and
dinghy sailing. Resorts that are particularly well
equipped for watersports activities include
Marmaris, Bodrum, Bitez, Kusadası , Kemer
and Foça.

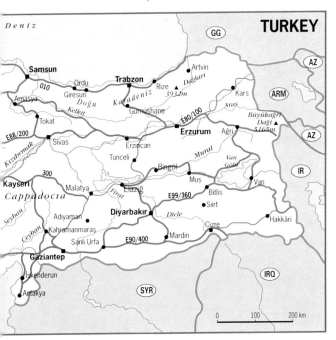

Sailing holidays along Turkey's Aegean and Mediterranean coasts are also in enormous demand now, especially aboard the traditional Turkish wooden boats known as *gulets* or ketches. These are made by craftsmen in boatyards located along the two coasts, and are specially designed for coastal cruising. Particularly popular are the itineraries known as 'Blue Voyage'.

Walking and trekking can be a real delight in Turkey, especially near Kemer and Alanya, while birdwatchers are also being increasingly catered for by the holiday companies.

A growing number of visitors are also discovering Turkey's thermal spas, long enjoyed by Turks themselves for their therapeutic and healing powers. Top resorts include Bursa, Çesme, Pamukkale and Yalova.

What to expect

The very fact that Turkey is relatively new to the mass holiday business means that standards are often not what visitors may have come to expect. The overall standard of public utilities, hygiene, drainage and services, for instance, are usually rather less sophisticated than those found in many other holiday countries. As an example, visitors should be prepared for Turkish-style bathrooms where the shower water drains away through a simple hole set in the middle of the floor – but only after flooding the bathroom first! Hot water cannot always be guaranteed, and water shortages in the peak summer months frequently occur.

Most Turkish hotels are clean and reasonably well equipped, but while the majority offer bedrooms with European-style furnishing, visitors opting for lower grade hotels and *pensions* should not be surprised if they are confronted with a row of pegs on the wall, instead of a wardrobe, since traditionally the Turks do not use wardrobes. Another point to bear in mind is that bedrooms, especially in the older-style hotels and self-catering apartments, are usually very small.

Outside the main resorts, there are numerous unmade, unlit roads, often little more than dirt tracks, leading to new holiday developments, so it is wise to take a torch with you for use in the

Away from the modern, cosmopolitan cities and resorts, life in Turkey continues much as it has always done

evenings. Because many of the resorts are expanding, building work is an ongoing activity, and the peace and quiet of a holiday can by no means be assumed.

Another disconcerting trend is for the provision of unnecessarily loud music at practically every open-air bar, restaurant or *lokanta,* no matter how peaceful and idyllic the setting.

No holiday destination, however, is without its drawbacks, and the inconveniences the visitor to Turkey is likely to experience pale into insignificance compared with the delights that lie in store: the superb weather, beaches, food, memorable excursions, the friendliness of a people for whom hospitality is a way of life, and the amazing value for money.

In this book, where appropriate, hotels and restaurants which enjoy good reputations are mentioned; the listings are selective rather than comprehensive, for the simple reason that Turkey's holiday industry is developing at a tremendous pace, with new establishments entering the field practically every day, especially in the up-and-coming coastal resorts. Those listed are generally well established, and usually offer reliable standards.

Likewise, the information given for motorists is not as comprehensive as that in guidebooks for many other popular holiday destinations, again for the simple reason that travel to Turkey by car is a mammoth undertaking for all but the most

INTRODUCTION

Istanbul's enormous covered market, the Covered Bazaar, a vast labyrinth of narrow passages containing between 4,000 and 6,000 little shops, was first created in the 15th century

intrepid. Car hire within Turkey is, however, growing in popularity, despite its high cost, so there are helpful tips for those who fancy picking up a car on arrival or hiring one for a few days. The majority of holiday-makers awakening to Turkey's attractions head for the resorts on her Aegean and Mediterranean shores, where the facilities and amenities are of a sufficiently high standard overall to ensure an enjoyable holiday. For this reason, greater prominence is given to resorts in these areas rather than those on Turkey's Black Sea coast which, though attractive and having much to offer the visitor, is comparatively underdeveloped when it comes to international tourism and, on the whole, lacks the type of facilities today's holiday-makers have come to expect.

Though developing at a rate, and in a manner, that many holiday-makers regret, Turkey nonetheless offers the chance to relax on comparatively uncrowded beaches, swim in secluded coves, feast on world-renowned cuisine, enjoy spectacular scenery, search for bargains in colourful shops and bazaars, or simply soak up the atmosphere of a western land with one face turned east.

THE AEGEAN COAST

Turkey's lovely Aegean region offers something for everyone – sun-lover, nature-lover, photographer, sightseer. Its shores abound in sandy beaches, sheltered coves and rocky bays lapped by blue, clean, crystal waters, and it is here that you will find some of the most popular, longest established and most picturesque resorts in the whole country – such as Bodrum, Marmaris and Kusadası – as well as brand new but fast-developing beach resorts such as Altınkum, with its beautiful golden sands.

The coast is also richly adorned with pretty fishing villages and the remains of many once-great cities. Here lie the ruins of the great city of Pergamon (now known as Bergama), which possessed one of the largest libraries in the ancient world, containing 200,000 volumes. Not far from Pergamon's acropolis are the ruins of one of the most important medical centres of the Classical world.

Further south is the capital of the Turkish Aegean, Izmir, the birthplace of Homer. This modern city with its palm-lined avenues and excellent hotels, boasts one of the finest natural harbours in Turkey. To the north of Izmir is the resort of Ayvalık, with lovely beaches and pine forests, and the little resort of Foça, whose inhabitants found and colonised such towns as Marseilles and Nice. West of Izmir lies the bigger and more developed resort of Çesme, with its thermal springs and yacht

4th century BC architects of the Temple of Apollo at Didim intended it to be the Eighth Wonder of the World

marina, while to the south of Izmir is Kusadası, one of the region's premier resorts, conveniently located for sightseeing and excursions to the many classical sites in the area. In the centre of Turkey's west coast is the region of ancient Ionia, boasting such ruins as Ephesus, Miletos and Didim, all reflecting the timeless grace of Ionian architecture. Chief among these Ionian cities is Ephesus, one-time Roman capital of Asia, and of which St Paul once asked 'Is there a greater city?' Along Ephesus' Arcadian Way, Mark Antony and Cleopatra once rode in procession; in the city's great theatre St Paul preached against the goddess Artemis; and in a little house outside the city the Virgin Mary is believed to have spent her last days. Also in Ephesus stood one of the Seven

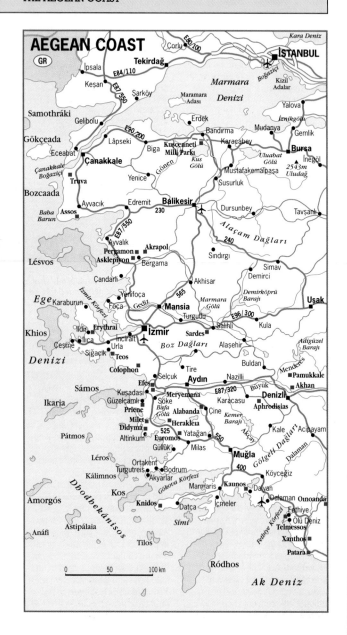

Wonders of the Ancient World, the Temple of Artemis.

In addition to these splendid man-made wonders, the Turkish Aegean offers a rich assortment of natural wonders, not least the calcified waterfall of Pamukkale, known as 'Cotton Castle', where thermal spring water laden with calcium carbonate running off the plateau's edge has formed a sparkling white petrified cascade of basins ringed by stalactites. Behind the waterfall lie the ruins of the once great Roman city of Hierapolis.

On the southwest of the Aegean coast are the popular resorts of Bodrum, Marmaris, Datça, Fethiye and Dalyan.

The hot summer temperatures that are a feature of Turkey's Aegean coast are tempered by gentle, refreshing sea breezes, while the rugged landscape is surprisingly green and luxuriant with fig orchards and olive groves.

ALTINKUM

Only a few years ago Altınkum was just a small hamlet located behind a wide sandy bay. Today, it is developing into one of Turkey's most popular, purpose-built beach resorts, with a good choice of new accommodation and no shortage of *lokantas,* cafés, bars and lively night-time diversions for when sunlovers have had enough of the resort's principal attraction, its magnificent beach.

At one end of the bay is a rocky headland, and beyond it is a series of coves backed by unspoilt, verdant countryside. Another cove at the other end is

sheltered and with fine sand; about ½ mile (0.8km) beyond is yet another series of fine sandy bays, all small, peaceful and unpolluted. Watersports lovers are particularly well catered for in Altınkum, with inexpensive professional instruction in windsurfing and other activities. Conditions are excellent for both beginners and the more experienced, the water being shallow and usually warm. Good value *lokantas,* ice cream parlours, bars and shops are to be found fronting the main bay for most of its length. Competition among the many small restaurants is fierce, so it is difficult to spend more than a trifling amount on a meal, and a sumptuous one at that!

Hotels and Restaurants

Among the best hotels in the resort are the 60-room **Gökkusagi**, with two swimming pools and good all-round amenities, and the 68-room **Tuntas**, which has a children's playground. In the medium-price category the 84-room **Göc** has no swimming pool but has a pleasant outdoor restaurant. Of the smaller, simpler hotels, the **Üç Mevsim**, about ten minutes' walk from the beach, has a colourful small terrace on which breakfasts are served and where barbecues are a regular feature.

Excursion from Altınkum

DIDIM

Only a few miles/kilometres from Altınkum, Didim was once called Didyma, and it was here that the ancient Greeks built a magnificent temple to Apollo, twin brother of Artemis. The original temple was destroyed by the Persians in 494BC and remained in ruins until Seleucus I of Syria began its restoration 200 years later, a feat that took no fewer than 600 years to accomplish, and even then not entirely.

Didyma itself was never a city but the site of a famous oracle, who was consulted by everyone from beggars to emperors. Unseen by anyone but the temple priests, the oracle would fast for three days and breathe the vapours emanating from the sacred spring. This seemingly put her in a state of divine inspiration, whereupon she passed obscure messages to the priests who, in turn, translated them for their clients. Oracles flourished at Didyma until the Byzantines adopted Christianity as the state religion.

Of the numerous remains, the most impressive are of the Temple of Apollo, its entrance marked by a lion. A monumental stairway leads up to a forest of 103 remarkably well-preserved Ionian columns.

End of excursion

◆◆◆
AYVALIK

Ayvalık is charmingly situated, with some 23 islands nestling in its bay and a coastline edged with pine forests and heavily indented with attractive coves. A walk through its twisting, high-walled streets is like stepping back in time, with tantalising glimpses through open doors to marble workshops and carpenters at work.

Architecture is an intricate blend of colours and designs, the skyline broken by chimneys and minarets – twin symbols of the dual nature of a traditional fishing town that also relies on light industry for its survival. Ayvalık has long been a popular holiday spot with Turkish visitors, and is now attracting increasing numbers of visitors from other countries.

Beaches
There are places to swim in and around the town, but some five miles (8km) or so south from the centre is Sarımsaklı – an attractive stretch of beach lined with hotels and café-bars.

Hotels and Restaurants
The luxury-class **Grand Hotel Temizel** offers a huge range of facilities, including indoor and outdoor restaurants, a cafeteria, pool and playground, disco, six bars, casino, nightclub, sauna and Turkish bath and many sports amenities. Cheaper, but good value, are the 61-room **Club Berk**, with two swimming pools, and the massive **Club Hotel Murat Reis**. Among the cheaper hotels in and around the town, the **Billurcu**, **Büyük Berk** and **Soley** are recommended. Ayvalık also offers a good choice of restaurants, but most visitors venture at least once to sample the seafood specialities of the restaurants of Alibey Adası, an island just across the bay, linked by a causeway. The charming waterfront has a small harbour with gaily painted boats and fringed with restaurants, some offering live entertainment.
Tourism Bureau: Yat Limanı Karşısı (tel: (663) 12122).

◆◆◆
BODRUM ✓

Bodrum is one of Turkey's best known and longest established holiday resorts, noted for its excellent facilities and amenities, cosmopolitan atmosphere and lively nightlife. A picture-postcard resort often referred to as the St Tropez of the eastern Aegean, it is very popular with younger holiday-makers, though its wide range of restaurants, shops, bars and discos, colourful and lively port and yacht marina, appeal to all age groups.

The ancient name of Bodrum was Halicarnassus, and it was founded in the 5th century BC as one of the great colonies of Greece. Its most famous citizen was Heredotus, the Father of History, born here in 485BC. The golden age of Halicarnassus occurred in the 4th century BC, when the ruling king of the region, Mausolus of Caria, made the town his capital. When he died, his wife-sister Artemisia succeeded him and built a memorial to her husband so vast and elaborate that it was subsequently declared one of the Seven Wonders of the Ancient World. Little remains of the structure, but the original site of the mausoleum can be seen on the outskirts of the town.

The town has a distinctly laid-back atmosphere, and one has the feeling that here, unlike anywhere else in Turkey, practically 'anything goes'. Despite the absence of notable beaches in the resort itself, its beautiful setting has led to the development of lively, modern tourist facilities. Yet in spite of its

Bodrum has been popular with holiday-makers for years

THE AEGEAN COAST

development, with new hotels and holiday apartments springing up practically overnight, it still manages to retain a distinct village charm. Tiers of dazzling cube-shaped, whitewashed houses ablaze with a profusion of flowers rise up from the harbour, where floating gin palaces jostle with quaint fishing boats and the stylish *gulet* wooden boats, built here in the resort.

Castle

The focal point is the magnificent 15th-century castle of St Peter, perched on a promontory dividing the two bays around which the town is set. Now housing a museum and open-air theatre, it is a treasure trove of the fruits of salvage operations off the local coast, some of which date back a thousand years. Construction of the castle began some time after 1402 when Tamerlane took the city and the Knights of St John consequently lost their fortress there.

The castle's five towers and the gothic chapel have all been carefully restored. The English Tower has been furnished with reproductions of tapestries, furniture, weapons and armour of the 15th century, giving the visitor an excellent idea of the life of those times.

The courtyards are adorned with ancient species of plants and trees and peacocks strut amid oleanders and statues.

The French and Italian Towers and the gothic chapel are used as archaeological museums, displaying objects taken from local sites. The best known of the museums, that of Underwater Archaeology, contains valuable

The Crusaders' impressive castle dominates the beautifully-sited port of Bodrum, formerly Halicarnassus, founded by Dorian Greeks

objects recovered since 1968 from expeditions in the Aegean and Mediterranean Seas. There are pieces of the hull and parts of the cargo of a Byzantine ship that sank about AD620; the wreck of a Bronze Age ship which went down about 1200 or 1300BC; and the wreck of an Islamic ship which was loaded with glass.

selling fine leather, jewellery and beachwear. At any time of the day or night there is always something going on here.

Beaches
The town beach is, to put it mildly, uninspiring. As compensation, from the colourful and elegant yacht harbour you can catch a boat to one of the many lovely coves near by – some of them practically deserted – or you can take a *dolmus* taxi to the sandy beaches of numerous little developing resorts such as Gümbet or Ortakent, only a short distance away round the bay.

Boat Trips
One of the best boat trips is a day exploring nearby Orak island, where fantastically clear water offers marvellous swimming and snorkelling. The boats continue on to Karaada, where you can bathe in beautifully warm sulphur springs. Do not miss the breathtakingly lovely Gulf of Gökova and the scenic serpentine route along the Datça peninsula, while in high season you can visit the Greek island of Kos for the day.

Mausoleum
Just round the corner from the castle are the remains of the first ever mausoleum, built in 376BC. Much of this Wonder of the Ancient World was dismantled by one of its earliest visitors, Sir Charles Newton, and shipped to the British Museum in London.

Bazaar
On the other side of the castle is Bodrum's own bazaar, a narrow street featuring scores of restaurants and bars, tiny shops

Hotels
The 85-room **Boydas** is only about 1¼ miles (2km) from Bodrum, and offers a good range of facilities that include indoor and outdoor restaurants, a swimming pool and several bars. The **Ayaz**, which is also close to the town, also has a good choice of facilities, as do the centrally situated 84-room **Blue Hotel** and 60-room **Bodrum Maya**. Of the many holiday villages along the bay, **Club Monakus** and the

THE AEGEAN COAST

long-established **Milta Torba** and **TMT** enjoy excellent reputations. Recommended hotels for those on a tighter budget include the 35-room **Aydem**, at Turgutreis, with a private beach but no swimming pool; and the 34-room **Makumba**, at Bitez, which has two pools and indoor and outdoor restaurants. Also to be recommended is the **Manastır**, constructed from the ruins of an old monastery, high on a hill overlooking the marina.

Discothèques
Bodrum is renowned for its nightlife. Of its many

Bodrum has developed into a lively modern resort catering for the tourist's every need, including all manner of souvenirs

discothèques, the one which stands out most is the **Halikarnas,** built in the form of an amphitheatre by the sea. As night progresses the Halikarnas lights up quite literally, with lasers projecting a spectacular display over the bay. One of the most sophisticated night spots in the whole of Turkey, it is a big hit with the young and trendy. There is a weekly folklore show here, with Turkish cuisine, folk performances and belly dancing. **Tourism Bureau**: 12 Eylül Meydanı (tel: (6141) 11091). On the main harbour square, near the castle wall.

Bodrum Peninsula
Bodrum's ever-growing popularity as a holiday resort has been seized upon by many of the

small beach settlements dotting the large peninsula on which it is located. As a result, many holiday-makers are choosing to stay in these fast developing small resorts, taking *dolmus* taxis into Bodrum for sightseeing or night-time diversions; while there is a constant flow of traffic in the opposite direction, with Bodrum-based holiday-makers spending the day on the beaches of the little resorts, and returning to Bodrum in the late afternoon. Distances obviously vary, but it usually takes about 10 minutes from Gümbet to Bodrum, or half an hour from the more outlying resorts.

Gümbet

Gümbet is the closest beach resort, and has plenty to offer families, couples and groups. It has a relaxed, easy-going ambience, with a long stretch of coarse, golden sand shelving gently into a warm sea, making it a great favourite with children and younger holiday-makers. The pensions, hotels and bars which line the beach offer sunshades and loungers, and many of them have colourful gardens where you can relax with a beer or a glass of tea. The afternoon breeze provides good windsurfing conditions and there is no shortage of opportunities to learn or improve your skills at this or at waterskiing, sailing or even scuba diving. Dinghies, canoes and pedaloes are also available for hire, and are not expensive.

Turgutreis

Turgutreis is another fast expanding beach resort whose growing popularity owes not a little to the fact that it is only 12 miles (19km) from Bodrum. It is also popular with holiday-makers who appreciate the opportunity of getting a little closer to the Turkish people, for here you encounter farmers, fishermen and weavers all going about their daily work, and wizened old men sitting at shaded tables drinking tea, playing cards and gossiping. On the long, clean beach there are loungers and sombrero-styled sunshades to rent, while for a change of pace there are the distractions of a town square, a playground and a market.

The approach to Turgutreis from Bodrum is particularly pleasant, since it enjoys a delightful green setting encircling a bay marked with islands. Named after Turgut Reis, who was born here and later became a Turkish admiral during the 16th century, the resort is, after Bodrum, the next largest settlement on the peninsula.

On the small waterfront promenade down by the square there are seats where you can sit over a drink while you admire the view across the bay. From the harbour, which is dotted with fishing boats, you can join a boat trip to the other areas of the peninsula or to Rabbit Island.

Ortakent

Ortakent is a charming, small seaside resort on the Bodrum peninsula, in a countryside setting of fig, orange and mandarin orchards. Wandering through the village you will see some fine examples of older-style Turkish architecture – such as the Mustafa Pasa Tower which

THE AEGEAN COAST

Although it has a lot to offer in the way of sailing and other watersports, Bitez remains quiet and unspoilt

was built in 1601 – while crowning the hill like sentinels as they gaze out to sea are old windmills.

A partly shaded road runs through the village for a little less than a mile (1.6km) before ending at the beach, a fairly long stretch of sand and pebbles bathed by calm waters. Here you can windsurf, hire a canoe or join an organised boat trip to a secluded bay or cove. Along the beach here are a couple of boat-building yards with builders at work – a craft which has been passed on down through generations.

Shopping requirements are catered for in a few mini-markets in the village, while for a change of pace, scenery and atmosphere the sophisticated attractions of Bodrum Town are within easy reach by *dolmus* taxi.

Bitez

Bitez is a rural, quiet and unsophisticated beach resort where small hotels, *pensions* and bars line the shingle and sand shore, and there are numerous small jetties for swimming and sunbathing. If you want to try your hand at windsurfing, this is one of the places for you – brightly coloured sails stretch out on the sand and water as far as the eye can see. Behind the beach, a short walk away, a tangle of small lanes winding through tangerine groves offer a picturesque alternative to lazing on the beach.

Akyarlar

A former fishing hamlet about half an hour's drive from Bodrum, Akyarlar comprises a few houses, hotels, *pensions*, grocery shops and bars, and remains a relatively 'get-away-from-it' retreat recommended for its comparative tranquillity and friendly atmosphere.

Along the road which runs on from Turgutreis to Akyarlar is a series of small bays and uncrowded beaches. The narrow strip of beach near the tiny harbour just below the village of Akyarlar shelves gently, while just around the bay is 'Black Fig' beach and a beach-side restaurant: a popular spot for pleasure crafts and day-trippers. There are organised boat trips from the village to neighbouring resorts, and Bodrum Town can be reached via Turgutreis.

Gölköy

A small farming community and beach resort, Gölköy stretches along the shore of a little-known bay about 20 minutes north of Bodrum by *dolmus* taxi and is a good base from which to visit other delightful bays around the peninsula. One of the chief attractions of Gölköy is its village atmosphere, with the possibility of quiet walks among old farm buildings and the opportunity of living among a mainly Turkish community away from crowds and mass tourism.

Güvercinlik

Güvercinlik, which means 'the place where doves come to roost', is another small unsophisticated resort nestling in a sheltered bay about 15 miles (24km) from Bodrum. Facilities in the resort include a general store, post office and a fruit and vegetable stall. There are no real beaches here, but swimming from the jetty is popular. Just a few miles/kilometres west of the resort are numerous little coves indenting this beautiful stretch of coastline, which are ideal for escapists and families in search of peace and quiet.

ÇESME

Çesme is one of Turkey's premier holiday resorts and one of its longest established. In the centre, little tumbledown houses are tucked away in quaint streets and alleyways which run behind the harbour, and here shoemakers, carpenters and tailors follow their trade much as they did in days gone by, while there are dozens of tiny shops in which to browse.

A resort with plenty of character, Çesme is dominated by a 14th-century fortress from which there are excellent views over the harbour.

In the resort's main square the jet black statues of Hasan Pasa and the lion that symbolises his temperament stare out to sea and to the Greek island of Chios, their backs to the impressive old fortress. The smooth round walls of this Genoese stronghold butt out into the pavement of the seafront road, where a multitude of waterfront restaurants vie for trade.

During the day a small sandy cove near the harbour is a suntrap for those who do not feel inclined to catch a *dolmus* taxi to the golden sands of Altınkum, only 4 miles (6.4km) away; or to one of the best beaches in the area, on the Ilıca road, just over a mile (1.6km) away. This wide, isolated strip of soft sand stretches for miles/kilometres and is seldom crowded. Its namesake, Ilıca, is a pretty marina town famed for its hot thermal baths; in fact, the name Çesme literally means 'fountain' or 'spring'.

Another place to visit is Dalyan

Köy, a small fishing village much frequented by lovers of good seafood. The setting is romantic, and you can eat in restaurants right by the water's edge. Food lovers will also appreciate Çesme's speciality: *lokma*, piping hot doughnuts popular with the locals and eaten at both breakfast and tea.

In ancient times Çesme, or Kysus as it was then known, was one of the most important cities of Ionia and it has been a major medical treatment centre and an active travel and naval base for centuries. Today, Çesme and its surroundings, makes a living from tobacco, olives, citrus fruits and grape cultivation, fishing and, increasingly, from tourism. Indeed, one of Turkey's biggest holiday developments is located here: the vast Golden Dolphin Holiday Village.

Fortress of Çesme

The fortress was enlarged, and new towers added, during its restoration in 1508 by the Ottoman Sultan Beyazit II, son of Mehmet the Conqueror. The castle and the port provided protection for the trading ships and the navy against inclement weather and enemy attacks. The south gate of the fortress is a characteristic example of Ottoman architecture.

Museum of Ottoman Arms

Located inside the fortress, this museum contains an excellent exhibition of cannons, swords, armour, pistols and rifles, most gathered from collections at Topkapı Palace, Istanbul. A gold and silver encrusted rifle, once belonging to Sultan Abdulaziz, is a prize exhibit.

Caravanserai

Built in 1529 by the architect Omar, this two-storey inn which adjoins the fortress was converted into a hotel in 1986. It boasts a delightful courtyard restaurant with regular Turkish folklore performances.

Mausoleum

This 18th-century, hexagonally designed museum reflects the main characteristics of Ottoman mausoleum architecture.

Hotels and Restaurants

The enormous, 508-room **Golden Dolphin Holiday Village** is popular with visitors looking for plenty of amenities and facilities, as are the hotels **Boyalık Beach** and **Delmar**. Cheaper, but well recommended are the **Kanuni Kervansaray** and the **Çesme Marin,** by the marina. There is a good selection of restaurants and bars, while nightlife is varied and quite chic, with music bars as well as discothèques keeping things pulsating way into the night.

Tourism Bureau: Iskele Meydanı 8 (tel: (549) 26653). Located at the port landing stage.

Excursions from Çesme

ERYTHRAI

Fourteen miles (22km) northeast of Çesme, at Ildırı, are the ruins of Erythrai, another of the important Ionian cities. Founded on the coastline of a beautiful bay dotted with small islands, Erythrai was inhabited by Cretans and Pamphylians after the Trojan War, and although the people managed to hang onto their traditions, the city

eventually became part of the Ionian parliament before being overthrown by Basili de Genos. Later, the Persians attacked the city and brought about its collapse.

◆◆
SIGACIK

A detour from the Izmir–Çesme road to Seferihisar leads to the village of Sıgacık, a picturesque little port surrounded by fortified walls dating from the Genoese period. To the east of the Bay of Sıgacık is an attractive beach from which the site of ancient Teos is easily accessible.
End of excursions

◆◆◆
DALYAN DELTA

The Dalyan Delta has leapt into prominence in recent times because its sandbar is one of the

Attractive holiday apartments and villas crowd up the hillside overlooking the harbour in Çesme

last breeding grounds in Europe of the loggerhead turtle. In view of the area's outstanding beauty, it had been earmarked for tourist development, including the construction of several large hotels right where the rare turtles come ashore to lay their eggs. Thanks to pressure from conservationists, the developments have been 'revised' by the government. The delta is reached by boat from the nearby village of Dalyan and the most popular way of experiencing it to the full is to take one of the many organised day excursions that include a tour of the ancient city of Caunos and a swim in Lake Köycegiz.

THE AEGEAN COAST

Ancient Lycian cave-tombs, carved out of the rock, abound in Anatolia; these are at Dalyan

Hotels and Restaurants

The **Antik**, about 1¼ miles (2km) from Dalyan, is a stylishly designed and furnished 42-room hotel offering indoor, terrace and garden restaurants, two bars, a pool and a children's pool.
Tourism Bureau: Atatürk Kordonu 1, Köycegiz (tel: (6114) 1703). By the waterfront.

Excursion from Dalyan

CAUNOS

Although not as spectacular as the ruins at many historic sites in

Turkey, those at Caunos, reached by boat along the Dalyan Delta, are still impressive. They include a 20,000-seat theatre, affording tremendous views from the top, Roman baths and the circular foundations of a small temple or pool.
End of excursion

DATÇA

A picturesque fishing village situated west along the Datça peninsula where the Aegean merges with the Mediterranean, Datça is rapidly becoming a popular resort due to the many yachts calling there, and to the fact that there are splendid sandy beaches nearby.

The town has considerable charm and quite a cosmopolitan atmosphere, with a variety of hotels, restaurants and shops including a couple of antique shops specialising in old carpets and wall-coverings. Off shore is a popular cruising ground for dolphins, while adjoining the beach is a lagoon fed by a freshwater stream.

Hotels

The **Dorya** is superbly located, surrounded by lovely gardens. Also recommended is the **Club Datça Tatil Köyü**, which has a pool, disco, sauna, tennis courts and watersports.

Tourism Bureau: Iskele Mah, Hükümet Binası (tel: (6145) 3146).

Excursion from Datça

KNIDOS

Another of Datça's chief attractions is its proximity to the ancient ruins of Knidos, about 24 miles (38km) away. These have been allowed to decay but indicate the one-time importance of this huge city which was founded in 400BC and served as a natural refuge for sailors at the crucial point where the Aegean flows into the Mediterranean.

Knidos was a famous centre of art, birthplace of the architect Sostratos who built one of the Seven Wonders of Antiquity, the lighthouse of Alexandria, and of the mathematician Eudoxus, who was the first to measure the earth's circumference.

Under Persian rule the city thrived as a trading centre, to such an extent that the harbour was unable to handle the increase in shipping. The city was then re-sited at the tip of the peninsula, a position which offered the benefit of two natural harbours. Excavations of the ruins were first begun in 1857 by Sir Charles Newton, who had everything of major interest unearthed and sent to the British Museum in London, including a statue of the goddess Demeter. Over the years the ruins have been repeatedly plundered, leaving only the foundations of temples, two theatres, an odeon and what is known as the lion tomb.

You can take a taxi from Datça to the nearest village, then walk the 3 miles (5km) to reach the site at the extreme tip of the peninsula.

THE AEGEAN COAST

The driver will wait for your return journey. A better alternative is a day-long boat trip from Datça that includes stops for swimming *en route*.

Boat excursions also operate to Datça from Bodrum, and there are coach or mini-bus trips from Marmaris.

End of excursion

FETHIYE

The lovely Gulf of Fethiye, its broad bay dotted with small islands and furrowed by inlets and coves, is one of the most impressive stretches of coastline in Turkey, its attractions greatly enhanced by lush, wooded mountain slopes which sweep down to the shore.

The town of Fethiye, which overlooks an attractive bay, is an ancient place crowned by the ruins of a fortress built by the Knights of Rhodes, and in the steep cliff surrounding it ancient Lycian tombs are carved out of the rock face. It is built on the site of ancient Telmessos, renowned for its wise scholars. Philip of Macedonia called on a sage from Telmessos to interpret a dream. This sage, Aristander, prophesised the birth and achievements of Alexander, and when the latter grew up the sage accompanied him on his campaigns.

Alexander took the city of Telmessos by trickery instead of force, asking the citizens to permit his musicians to enter. They agreed, and by night the musicians took over the city with spears and shields they had smuggled in. However, Alexander restored the city to its king out of respect for Aristander, leaving only one of his generals as the governor of Lycia.

Like the other Lycian cities, Telmessos was successively ruled by Egyptians, Syrians, Rhodians, Romans and Byzantines.

No excavations have been undertaken in the town itself, and few remains can be seen, since a severe earthquake completely destroyed both the ancient buildings and the Ottoman town in 1958. However, two Lycian tombs can be seen in the town, one beneath the rock tombs and another near the wharf.

Although architecturally uninspiring, Fethiye none the less has much to please the visitor. A wide promenade lined with cafés runs around its colourful harbour and small yachting marina, tables and chairs spilling out from underneath awnings and trees onto a waterfront terrace. Most of the daytime action centres around Fethiye's open market, a riot of colours, sounds and smells, where you can buy a wide range of goods and souvenirs, colourful Turkish slippers, handmade jewellery, leather goods and much more. Part fishing village and part market town, and situated close to beautiful countryside, Fethiye is a town full of local hustle and bustle, not exactly pretty, but certainly the sort of place that grows on you, with shops and restaurants primarily geared to locals rather than holiday-makers. The nearby coast is peppered with sandy bays.

Hotels and Restaurants

The **Likya** is well located and enjoys a reputation as one of the best hotels in town. Also good is the large **Aries Club**, which has a wide range of amenities. There is no shortage of places to eat, with many lively restaurants and bars in the back streets and alleys as well as on the seafront, and most offer a tempting range of dishes.

Tourism Bureau: Iskele Meydanı 1 (tel: (615) 41527). By the marina.

Çalis

Because Fethiye itself does not have a beach, that at Çalis, no more than 2½ miles (4km) away round the bay, has readily stepped into the gap, and the little resort has become a particular favourite for

The fascinating rock tombs near Fethiye are hewn out of a vertical cliff and have impressive façades

watersports. It offers a long, wide beach of coarse sand/shingle, cooled in the afternoons by a strong sea breeze which keeps the temperature pleasant even in the height of summer, and is perfect for windsurfing.

The beach is big enough to be seldom crowded, and is bordered by a road lined with cafés, restaurants, *pensions* and hotels, as well as a disco. Across the bay are lovely views of tiny, idyllic islands which face the coast, while majestic, lush green mountains behind give Çalis a special appeal.

The little resort offers a wide

The many remains at Xanthos give a good indication of that magnificent city's long and turbulent history

choice of restaurants and *lokantas* to satisfy most holiday-makers' requirements, while the attractions of lively Fethiye are only an inexpensive *dolmus* taxi hop away.

Excursions from Fethiye

Excursions from this area are many and varied. In and around Fethiye itself are the intriguing Lycian rock tombs carved into the cliff face, or you can venture off to see the ancient sites of Patara and Xanthos.

◆◆
PATARA

An excursion to Patara – about 50 miles (80km) from Fethiye – is worthwhile on two counts, for not only is it a site of great antiquity, but it also boasts one of the best, totally unspoilt beaches in Turkey.

Once a thriving port, Patara's greatest days where during the Roman period, when it was the principal harbour in Lycia. Most of the surviving ruins date from that period, and include a theatre. Patara has been declared a protected area by the Turkish government, which means that hotel development is severely restricted, and not allowed by the beach or near the ruins, the extent of which becomes clear as you scramble among the dunes of fine, pale sand.

◆◆
XANTHOS

The Persian army entered the plain of Xanthos under the command of Harpagos, and did battle with the Xanthians. The greatly outnumbered

Xanthians fought with legendary bravery against the superior Persian forces but were finally beaten and forced to retreat within the walls of their city, gathering their womenfolk, children, slaves and treasures into the fortress. This was then set on fire from below and around the walls, until destroyed by conflagration. Then the warriors of Xanthos made their final attack on the Persians, their voices raised in oaths of war, until every last man from Xanthos was killed.

Thus records Heredotus of Halicarnassus (Bodrum), and the fact that Sarpendon of Xanthos commanded Lycian troops in the Trojan War allows us to infer that Xanthos existed even earlier, in 1200BC.

This magnificent city, which lies about 40 miles (65km) from Fethiye, was rebuilt following its destruction at the hands of the Persians, but burned down once more between 475BC and 450BC, as indicated by a thick layer of ash discovered during excavations. After being ruled successively by Alexander the Great, the Ptolomeans and the Syrian monarch Antiochus III, Xanthos became the capital of the Lycian confederacy in the 2nd century BC.

The Romans demolished the Lycian acropolis and slaughtered the city's inhabitants, although the fact that a year later Marcus Antoninus had the city rebuilt and a monumental portal erected in the name of Emperor Vespasian indicates that relations with the Romans were later amicable. The city was abandoned during the Byzantine period after the first Arab incursion.

Xanthos was rediscovered in 1838 by an English archaeologist who had all the reliefs and archaeological finds of interest taken to London on a warship which sailed from Patara. Many works of art from the site are now on display in the Lycian room of the British Museum, London. The city dominated a green plain watered by the River Esen (Xanthos) and here can be seen many monuments from the Lycian, Roman and Byzantine periods.

Near the Roman theatre stand three splendid mausoleums: a Roman colonnaded tomb dating from the 1st century AD; a Lycian colonnaded tomb on a high base dating from the 4th century BC, on which was found the relief of a wrestler which predated the tomb itself; and the famous Tomb of the Harpies, whose original reliefs are now in the British Museum. Plastercasts taken from the originals have been replaced on the tomb. Near the theatre are the remains of a Byzantine church and a Lycian palace, and a little further on is the Lycian pool, hollowed out of the rock. The royal terrace situated at the extremity of the acropolis overlooks the entire plain.
End of excursions

FOÇA

A former pirate stronghold with an easygoing atmosphere, Foça is a quiet and attractive fishing town. A small shingle beach at one end of the bay is a popular sunspot, but the best swimming in the area can be found on the

THE AEGEAN COAST

white sandy beach only 2 miles (3.2km) along the coast. Foça was the ancient port of Phocaea and the northernmost Ionian settlement, noted for its harbour and seafaring men.

Hotels and Restaurants

Accommodation is confined to the large **Club Méditerranée** holiday village, which has the usual facilities.
Tourism Bureau: Atatürk Mah, Foça Girisi 1 (tel: (543) 11222).

Excursion from Foça

◆◆◆
PERGAMON

Within easy reach of the resort is the ancient site of Pergamon – one of the most impressive Classical sites in Turkey. It lies just outside the town of Bergama, where there is a good archaeological and ethnographical museum. Of particular interest to visitors is the library which once held 200,000 books, competing with that in Alexandria. It is said that Mark Antony creamed the best of the collection and gave it to Cleopatra.

During the city's greatest period, a gymnasium was built and also an altar to Zeus. More than a thousand figures, half animal and half human, were represented in a series of reliefs, celebrating the triumph of good over evil.

The theatre here has 80 tiers of seats capable of holding 10,000. Also impressive is the Asklepiyon, the ancient health centre which experimented in the healing powers of herbs and sacred waters. It was considered to be one of the finest centres of its kind in the world.
End of excursion

A romantic sunset across Izmir Bay

◆◆◆
IZMIR

Izmir is a pleasant city with palm-lined boulevards, a lively atmosphere, excellent hotels and shops, and plenty to interest the visitor, including first-rate seaside restaurants, museums, a cultural park, and a bazaar offering a wide variety of antiques, jewellery and clothing. Turkey's second largest port and her third largest city, with a population of approximately 2,350,000, it is impressively situated at the end of a large gulf ringed by mountains and, though not strictly speaking a holiday

colourful. Close to the bazaar are three attractive mosques, the Kemeraltı Camii, Hisar Camii and Sadirvan Camii, plus two 17th-century caravanserais.

Roman Agora
Not far from the bazaar are the imposing remains of the Roman agora (market place), dating from the 2nd century AD. Several portals lead on to the square, where you can see statues of Poseidon, Demeter and Artemis.

Velvet Castle
Kadifekale, the Velvet Castle, dominates Izmir from the top of Mount Pagos. It was on this mountain that, according to legend, Nemeses appeared to Alexander the Great in a dream and told him to found a city on this site and encourage the inhabitants of the old city of Izmir to move here. The original fortress was constructed by Lysimachus, one of Alexander the Great's generals, and it was later restored by the Romans and the Byzantines. From the castle there is a magnificent panorama of the city and bay.

Hotels and Restaurants
Recommended at the top of the range are the **Büyük Efes**, **Grand Plaza** and the **Etap Izmir**. In the medium price sector, the **Hisar**, **Izmir Palas** and **Kilim** represent value for money, while popular with those on a tight budget are the **Kabaçam** and **Kayalar**.
There are many restaurants on the waterfront, the **Deniz** being one of the best.
Tourism Bureau: Gazi Osman Pasa Bulvarı 1C, Büyük Efes Hotel (tel: (51) 899278/842147).

resort since it lacks a beach, it is a popular base for sightseeing. The city contains a few vestiges of its rich past, owing to a great fire that destroyed much of it in 1922, but there are many places of interest well worth visiting. If you leave from Cumhuriyet Meydanı (Republic Square), where there is an imposing statue of Atatürk, you can walk along Atatürk Caddesi, which runs along the seafront and is lined with restaurants, nightclubs and travel agencies. At Konak Meydanı there is an elegant clock-tower in the Moorish style. From here you can walk through the little streets to the bazaar, which is usually very lively and

Excursions from Izmir

Izmir is an ideal point of departure for many excursions, including trips to the historic sites of Ephesus (see page 37–8) and Aphrodisias (see page 42).

◆◆◆
KUSADASI

In the centre of Turkey's Aegean coast, in the region of ancient Ionia, lies Kusadası, the 'Island of Birds', surrounded by some of the richest historical sites in the world.

Kusadası's superb setting, pleasant beaches, colourful harbour and marina, pavement cafés, quayside restaurants and wide variety of shops have made the resort one of the Turkish Aegean's most popular holiday spots, although it was included in the Aegean itineraries of cruise ships long before the Turkish tourism boom started in earnest. Indeed, such is the popularity of this port town, with its easy access to the ruined city of Ephesus – a 'must' on any visitor's itinerary – that as many as eight ships a day call here during the high season. Despite considerable development and expansion in recent years the resort, which is opposite the Greek island of Samos, has managed to hold on to a great deal of its charm.

Beaches

Kusadası has two beaches: the none-too-inspiring town beach, and a much nicer one known as Kadinlar, or Ladies' Beach, about 2 miles (3.2km) from the harbour area. Here, fine powder sand stretches for about half a mile (0.8km), and is well served by *lokantas* and restaurants as well

as roving Turks offering anything from corn on the cob to chilled beer and soft drinks. Some of the better beaches in and around Kusadası are owned by hotel complexes, but the modest entrance fee is redeemable against drinks and snacks. The wide, clean promenade which separates the sea from the main avenue is a good spot for a pre-dinner or early morning stroll, while the resort's numerous attractions include an old caravanserai, now a stylish hotel with an attractive if relatively expensive courtyard restaurant.

Shopping

There are shady terraces throughout Kusadası where one can sit and sip *raki* or a glass of sweet Turkish tea. The main street is lined with little shops offering tempting bargains – anything and everything, including leatherwear, jewellery, brass, copper and onyx, as well as cheap tee-shirts.

Attractions

Kusadası's old quarter is a picturesque and atmospheric maze of winding streets, some rising steeply above the harbour, its houses adorned with colourful flowers and birdcages. In the lower street, just behind the seafront, are the majority of the shops.

On the little isle known as Güvercin Adası (Isle of Doves), which is joined to the mainland by a small jetty, is a fortress built by the Turks in the 14th or 15th century and said to have been a den of notorious pirates whose daring escapades were known throughout the Mediterranean.

Today, the gardens, and the disco inside the castle, are popular with holiday-makers, especially in the evenings when the sun is setting and the whole bay takes on a magical atmosphere.

Hotels and Restaurants

Kusadası offers an enormous choice of accommodation, from five-star hotels with excellent facilities, and holiday villages offering plenty of activity, to more modest hotels and simple pensions. Good, but relatively expensive, are the stylish 250-room **Korumar**, 276-room **Fantasia** and 330-room **Onur**, all of which have a wide range of amenities. Medium-price recommendations include the **Adakule**, **Batihan** and **Imbat**, and at the less expensive end of the scale the 35-room **Doridas**, which has a swimming pool with bar and both indoor and outdoor restaurants, as does the **Olmez**. **Öküz Mehmetpasa Kervansarayı** converted from the magnificent caravanserai (inn) built in 1618, is stylish if somewhat pricey. Of the holiday villages, the **Club Méditerranée** and **Sunset View** are probably the best. The 30-room **Diamond Pension** is a simply furnished, small budget hotel in a pleasant waterside location.

As well as a Turkish night held at Öküz Mehmetpasa Kervansarayı, complete with traditional Turkish food and belly dancing, there are literally hundreds of *lokantas* and restaurants, including one Chinese. If you want to find a good bar, look upward – Kusadası has more than its fair share of roofbars.

The old 17th-century caravanserai in Kusadası has been converted into a luxury hotel

The restaurants and bars at Kadinlar range from the thatched roof and fishing net variety with rickety tables, to smarter establishments such as the **Salmuk**, with live music. Kusadası is also rich in discos and many of the restaurants have live music at least once a week – a blessing or a curse depending on your point of view.

Tourism Bureau: Liman Caddesi (tel: (636) 11103). By the Customs Office at the landing stage.

Gulf of Kusadası

Güzelçamlı

The great sweep of the Gulf of Kusadası is broken up by small promontories into several bays fringed by long sandy beaches. And in one of these bays, about 16 miles (25.5km) from the centre of Kusadası, nestles the

THE AEGEAN COAST

small, unsophisticated but fast-developing resort of Güzelçamlı – a good choice for a relaxing, laid-back beach holiday with the bonus of Kusadası's big-resort attractions only a short and inexpensive *dolmus* taxi ride away. The resort, as yet unspoilt and typically Turkish, has sprung up round a pretty bay and its beach of coarse sand.

The old village, set a short distance from the beach, offers a range of small *lokantas*, bars and restaurants, and it is here that the *dolmus* taxis pick up passengers seeking the diversions of Kusadası.

Beaches

In addition to the resort's own beaches, there is another, more pleasant beach within walking distance, equipped with loungers and shades and also a beach bar. There are also two more

Ephesus – the almost-complete theatre in a theatrical setting

delightful beaches within the nearby Samsundag National Park, famous for its natural beauty and its delightful, uncrowded and unpolluted coves and beaches. All these beaches can be reached quite easily by *dolmus* taxi.

Excursions from Kusadası

Even those with little interest in history should not miss the opportunity of making an excursion to the magnificent ruins of Ephesus about half an hour from Kusadası, and one of Turkey's most impressive ancient sites. Most people reach Ephesus by joining one of the numerous excursions from Kusadası; but it is just as easy by *dolmus* taxi – the journey is about 7 miles (11km). In addition, there are excursions to the fascinating old Ionian cities of Priene and Miletos, while throughout the summer regular boat trips operate from Kusadası to the Greek island of Samos.

◆◆◆
EPHESUS ✓

Travellers who visited Ephesus in the early 19th century found nothing but a few cottages, and did not make even a passing reference to the place in their notes. Yet today, it is among the most famous historic sites in Turkey, and the most visited. The first excavations were undertaken in 1896 by Austrian archaeologists, and have since continued virtually uninterrupted. It is one of three cities planned by the architect Hippodamos, who lived in Miletos in the 4th century BC; the plan applied in Miletos was used subsequently in Ephesus and Priene. Known by some as the grid plan, it consists of intercrossing streets, the main roads lined by public buildings and temples, and the minor roads by private houses. From a vantage point on a hillside behind the city, the grid system of streets is clearly visible.

The three main roads are the Harbour Road or Arcadius, the Marble Road and Curette Road. Most of the buildings visible today are ranged along these three roads and almost all date from the Roman period.

On entering the city from the direction of the harbour the first building to strike the eye is the splendid amphitheatre on the slope of Panayir Dagi (Mountain). With a seating capacity of 24,000, this is the largest theatre in Anatolia. Originally built in the Hellenistic period, it was extensively altered by the Romans, and during Byzantine times much of the seating was removed and the stone used in other buildings.

Many of these have been recovered by archaeologists and the theatre today appears much as it did in Roman times.

At the junction of Marble Road and Curette Road, the façade of the Celsus Library, one of the finest examples of Roman period decoration, acts like a magnet. The building faces east so that the morning light entered the windows of the reading rooms. It was built by a rich Roman named Hulius Aquila in memory of his father Celsus, and its collection of books was one of the largest in the ancient world.

Further along Curette Road to the right can be seen the tiled houses of rich Ephesians, rising by stages on vaults and built in the form of a peristyle around a colonnaded courtyard. The ivory objects, valuable statuettes and frescos discovered when excavating these houses confirm that they were the homes of the rich and powerful. The brick pillars under the floors show that they had under-floor heating in the manner of Roman baths.

Of the famous Temple of Artemis, once one of the Seven Wonders of the Ancient World, unfortunately nothing but a single column remains. A Grecianised version of the far more ancient Anatolian goddess Cybele, the goddess of fertility, Artemis was worshipped in all Greek cities, but in Ephesus her importance was far more wide-ranging. The statue of Artemis in the Temple was believed to have been the gift of the Amazons or, according to another version of the story, to have come from heaven.

THE AEGEAN COAST

Not only did Artemis of Ephesus bring prosperity to the region but, the residents believed, she cured the sick, was a regulator of commercial life and protected the city from danger.

Such a generous goddess deserved extra special treatment in return, and a large retinue of priests, priestesses, temple virgins, attendants who dressed the statue of Artemis and musicians served at the Temple.

SELÇUK

The town of Selçuk, which lies just outside Ephesus, is dominated by a Byzantine fortress, once the largest temple in Asia Minor, surrounded by 129 marble columns, and also has a museum with interesting objects recovered from Ephesus, including a life-size figure of Artemis.

Tourism Bureau: Atatürk Mah, Agora Çarsısı 35, Selçuk (tel: (5451) 1328/1945). Opposite the museum.

MERYEMANA (HOUSE OF THE VIRGIN MARY)

On a site 4¼ miles (7km) above Selçük, now occupied by a small chapel, the Virgin Mary is said to have spent the last few years of her life. The site is now a place of pilgrimage.

PRIENE

Priene, perched high on a rock and now separated from the sea by 10 miles (16km) of alluvial plain, was one of the busiest ports of the Ionian Federation. What makes the site of particular interest is the system of geometric planning introduced in the 4th century BC by Hippodamos of Miletos. The theatre is the most interesting of Priene's remains; the lower tiers are virtually intact, and the whole theatre retains its original character. Only a few columns remain of the Temple of Athena, which was a classic example of Ionian architecture. Priene is about 30 miles (50km) south of Kusadası.

MILETOS (MILET)

Miletos, like Priene, was once a great Ionian port, with no fewer than four harbours, and the native city of several philosophers and sages. Most of the monuments at the site are badly ruined except for the theatre and the Baths of Faustina. The theatre, reconstructed during the Roman period, is an impressive building. Five columns of the once great Temple of Athena have been re-erected to give an indication of its original massive scale. Miletos is about 30 miles (50km) south of Kusadası.
End of excursions

MARMARIS

With its dramatic setting at the foot of pine-clad hills among some of Turkey's most staggeringly beautiful scenery, a relaxing atmosphere and excellent facilities and amenities, the picturesque, palm-filled resort of Marmaris is one of the most popular in the whole of Turkey. It is even a favourite holiday haunt of the Turks

An enterprising old gentleman and his weighing machine, Marmaris

by the Persians until Alexander the Great ousted them in 334BC. The Romans had conquered the region by 163BC, and after the division of the Roman Empire, the area fell until Byzantine rule. The region was wrested from the Byzantines in AD1282 by the Turkish Emir of Mentese, and in 1425 the rule of the Ottoman Turks was established.

Today, Marmaris is a well-equipped holiday resort with scores of excellent hotels and holiday villages, many of international standard, as well as numerous simpler but well-furnished smaller hotels, family-run *pensions*, and modern villas and apartments.

Dominating the scene is a medieval castle built by Sultan Süleyman the Magnificent on a hill behind the yacht harbour. In addition to its historic battlements, it offers great views.

themselves and, although its beach is nothing special, its popularity is not difficult to understand. The lovely fjord-like stretch of coastline where the Aegean meets the Mediterranean offers numerous unspoilt and practically deserted coves fringing a warm, turquoise-blue sea, making the area a good choice for those who enjoy sunbathing and seawater swimming.

Once the ancient port of Physus, occupying an important place on the commercial trading route between Anatolia, Rhodes and Egypt, Marmaris was part of the southwest Aegean kingdom of Caria, the two most powerful cities of which were Knidos and the capital, Bodrum. In the 6th century BC Caria fell to the Lydians and was then subjugated

Beaches

The best beaches are not in the resort itself, but further along the bay, all easily accessible by *dolmus* taxis. Best of all are those reached by boat: beautiful, practically deserted sandy coves popular for picnics or lazy days enjoying the sun, the sea and lovely setting. There is an impressive range of facilities for watersports lovers, with sailing, windsurfing and waterskiing all readily and inexpensively available, together with the latest craze, jet-skiing.

Boat *dolmus*, the water-borne equivalents of the taxis, go to the many beaches and islets round the bay, while regular ferry services operate to Rhodes, or you can join one of the main excursion programmes available. Details are available from the tourism bureau (see below). The harbour and marina area are particularly lively and colourful, teeming with fishing and pleasure boats and yachts, while the palm-fringed promenade has seats at regular intervals so you can sit and admire the beautiful bay or enjoy a cool drink or an ice cream from one of the kiosks.

Shopping

Marmaris is arguably the most attractive of Turkey's holiday resorts for shopping, with most shops in the streets leading off the seafront offering a good selection of goods and crafts. Many of them remain open well into the evening. Especially popular take-home gifts are jars of local honey, and sponges.

Hotels and Restaurants

Marmaris has an excellent range of quality hotels, *pensions* and self-catering accommodation. At the upper end of the scale both the **Altınyunus** and **Grand Azur** have good facilities. Recommended mid-price hotels include the **Pineta** and **Turunç**, which have large swimming pools; the **Amos Yacht Club** which, as the name implies, caters to those who enjoy messing about in boats; and the **Lidya**, one of the best located hotels in the resort, set amid lovely tropical gardens. Less expensive hotels enjoying good reputations include the **Hawaii** and the **Marmaris**.

There is also a good choice of restaurants, as well as enticing pastry shops, bars – one of the most popular is the **Daily News** – and several lively discos.
Tourism Bureau: Iskele Meydanı 92 (tel: (612) 21035), Next to the Customs Office at the harbour.

Içmeler

As Marmaris becomes more popular, Içmeler is developing into a resort in its own right thanks to an attractive bronze sandy beach stretching for about half a mile (0.8km). The sea here is warm, clear and pollution-free – a boon for swimmers and windsurfers. Watersports equipment, including jet-skis, are available for hire, as are beach loungers and sunshades. Although it is becoming increasingly popular, Içmeler has retained much of its unspoilt small-resort appeal, and is ideal for a quiet, relaxing and unsophisticated beach holiday amidst lovely scenery.
The village itself offers a selection of small general stores, fruit and vegetable stalls, bars and *lokantas*, and a choice of simple, ethnic restaurants. There is even a disco whose popularity is such that it attracts customers from its much bigger and much more sophisticated neighbour Marmaris.

Hotels

The **Nunamar** is large and somewhat uninspiring in appearance, but its amenities include pools for adults and children, four bars, saunas and Turkish bath, shops and varied sports facilities. Mid-price recommendations are the **Blue Rainbow**, **Club Atlantik** and the **Private**, while for those on a budget the **Kanarya** is good value, with a large pool and children's pool. The long-established **Martı II** holiday village is one of the best in Turkey, with an excellent setting and a good range of facilities.

Excursions from Marmaris

As a base for sightseeing, either by water or road, Marmaris is well situated. Treasures such as the ancient Lycian tombs carved into the rock face at Fethiye and Ölu Deniz, with its white sandy beaches and inviting sea, are both within fairly easy reach, as are Pamukkale, and the ancient site of Aphrodisias.

Islands: For a pleasant day out, Paradise Island is totally uncommercialised except for one simple *lokanta*. Excursions also operate to Cleopatra's Island.

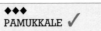

♦♦♦ PAMUKKALE ✓

Pamukkale is one of the many jewels in the Turkish tourism crown. The word meaning 'cotton castle' is a fitting description. The waters of thermal springs laden with calcium carbonate have formed a dazzling white petrified cascade of stalactites, flowing over the plateau's edge into a series of basins and pools. It is best reached by bus or train to Denizli, then *dolmus* taxi for about 10½ miles (17km).

At night at Pamukkale the pools of water overflow into each other down the cliffs, adding more calcium to the enormous stalactites that fringe them

THE AEGEAN COAST

Tourism Bureau: Örenyeri, Pamukkale (tel: (6218) 1077).

♦♦♦
HIERAPOLIS

On top of the plateau are the ruins of ancient Hierapolis, founded in the 2nd century BC and among whose ancient buildings are the thermal baths, part of which now form a museum of sculpture. The site also includes a Christian basilica, Temple of Apollo, theatre and Martyrium of the Apostle, Philip, who was martyred here in AD80.

♦♦♦
APHRODISIAS

The ruins of Aphrodisias, at the foot of the Baba Dag Mountains, form one of the most important and attractive archaeological sites in Turkey.

The city was the centre of the cult of Aphrodite and a flourishing school of sculpture, but it reached its zenith during the Roman period. Aphrodisias' huge stadium, which could accommodate 30,000 spectators, is one of the best preserved in the Roman world. Fourteen elegant columns remain standing of the Temple of Aphrodite, which was a pilgrimage centre and a place of sanctuary. Near the Temple is a beautiful gateway, and there is also a small odeon or concert hall, with an elaborately decorated stage. Several Ionic porticos and twelve columns remain of the agora or marketplace. Also of interest are the thermal baths of Hadrian and two palatial residences. Fine sculptures are displayed in the museum in nearby Geyre.
End of excursions

With a setting like this, no wonder Ölü Deniz is a favourite holiday spot

♦♦♦
ÖLÜ DENIZ

Ölü Deniz offers one of the most spectacular and beautiful beaches in the whole of Turkey, with a magnificent crescent of dazzling pale sand fringing a clear, pollution-free lagoon of turquoise blue. Set in an area of outstanding natural beauty (a nature park) the lagoon is almost entirely cut off from the sea – perfect for safe swimming and watersports. Located about 10 miles (16km) from the ancient port and resort of Fethiye, tourist development has mercifully

small charge is made to enter this area in order that litter bins can be provided and the place is kept clean and tidy.

Hotels
Closest to the delightful beaches of Ölü Deniz are the 75-room **Meri**, superbly located but with varying standards; and the newer 126-room **Ölü Deniz** holiday village, with indoor and outdoor restaurants, five bars, two swimming pools, nightclub, shops and excellent sports facilities. Apart from these, most of the holiday accommodation is located a few miles/kilometres inland in the tiny villages of Ovacik and Hisaronu, leaving the beach area around Ölü Deniz delightfully unspoilt.
Ovacik is about a five minute journey by *dolmus* taxi from Ölü Deniz, and is an attractive little development of small *pensions*, hotels and *lokantas*, set in delightful countryside.
Hisaronu, likewise, is only a few miles/kilometres from Ölü Deniz, and is also surrounded by lush green countryside and fruit orchards. It boasts a pleasant hotel, the **Suzanne** which provides clean, comfortable accommodation and is well-run. For something really different in the way of accommodation, try the obscure but picturesque village of **Ocakkoy**, which lies between Ölü Deniz and Fethiye. A twisting track leads through a pine forest to this small settlement of stone houses built on the slopes of a hill and surrounded by pine woods. The village, abandoned by the Greeks some 60 years ago, comprises a selection of one-

been severely restricted. The main beach at Ölü Deniz is fronted by a few bars and *lokantas* that offer excellent variety at ridiculously low prices. At one end of the bay a thickly wooded peninsula forms one arm of the lagoon. The landward side of the lagoon has a beach of fine golden sand. There are delightful boat trips to deserted islands and to a fascinating fish farm, and beach barbecues are a feature of this resort.
The countryside around Ölü Deniz is also well worth exploring. There is even a delightful area set within the nature park that is equipped with tables and chairs in the woods that run down to the beach. A

THE AEGEAN COAST

bedroom houses, furnished with antiques, richly patterned rugs and *kilims*, and with modern bathrooms, plus a motel section. Owned by a Turkish sea-captain and his English wife, the village also has a small restaurant, outdoor bar, swimming pool, tennis court, shop and a pottery and enjoys a magnificent view over the valley. The owners run a daily mini-bus service to Ölü Deniz and to Fethiye.

Restaurants

There are several restaurants and bars near the beach at Ölü Deniz, and even a couple of small discos and a stylish and sophisticated new restaurant built on the very edge of the cliffs that form Ölü Deniz Bay. There is also a reasonable choice of hotel restaurants and bars in both Ovacik and Hisaronu, as well as small *lokantas*. Fethiye, with its more sophisticated tourist amenities is only a short *dolmus* drive away.

HOW TO GET TO THE AEGEAN

By Air

Holiday resorts on the Turkish Aegean coast are served by two principal airports, Izmir and Dalaman. A new domestic airport is planned for Bodrum; there are, however, regular shuttle services from Izmir and Dalaman to Bodrum Stolport.

Izmir (Adnan Menderes) Airport has direct scheduled and charter services from many European cities. Coaches transfer beach holiday-makers to their chosen resort. Several of these are easily

reached from Izmir, including Foça, to the northwest, Çesme, due west, and Kusadası. Fly-drive holiday-makers pick up their cars at the airport or at their overnight hotel. Many coach tours around Turkey have Izmir as their starting point.

Dalaman Airport first opened for charter flights in 1982 and has since been extended to cope with the increasing number of flights here from major European cities. It has a 24-hour taxi service as well as car rental facilities. Approximate distances by road to some of the nearest resorts are: Dalyan 19 miles (30km), Fethiye 39 miles (63km), Marmaris 65 miles (105km) and Bodrum 132 miles (213km). Coach services operate from Dalaman Town to Marmaris, between 07.00 and 18.15hrs (75 minutes); Bodrum at 11.00 and 13.30hrs (3 hours); and Fethiye, hourly or more frequently during the peak holiday period (1 hour).

By Boat

Turkish Maritime Lines' boats leave Istanbul regularly, stopping at ports along the Aegean coast. There are also frequent services to Izmir from Marseilles and Genoa, and car-ferry links in the summer from Venice and Brindisi.

By Road

The car journey across Europe is long, sometimes tedious and, in parts, not at all easy. Motorists from western Europe can remove up to 500 miles (800km) from their journey by using the Greek port of Piraeus and taking a car ferry to the Turkish Aegean ports.

THE MEDITERRANEAN

Known as the Turkish Riviera, or the Turquoise Coast, the Mediterranean region of Turkey has much to offer the holiday-maker, including a delightful climate even in the winter months, long stretches of fine, sandy beach, excellent hotels, a good range of sightseeing options and plenty of value-for-money restaurants.

The whole coast is rich in legend and history, with many ruins of ancient cities, theatres and great Crusader castles. Tourist office literature boasts that Mark Antony once gave part of these shores to Cleopatra as a wedding gift, and whether the legend is true or not, there can be no denying that the shoreline is exceedingly attractive, with seemingly endless stretches of white sand set against the often snow-capped peaks of the Taurus Mountains. The verdant shores are covered with pine forests, orange groves and banana plantations, splashed here and there with the vivid pink of wild oleanders, as well as mushrooming hotels and holiday villages.

The principal resorts are Antalya, magnificently situated on the shores of a broad bay; Side, located between two vast stretches of sandy beach next to the ruins of an ancient city; Kemer, a 20-mile (32km) stretch of sand/pebble beach among pine woods and citrus groves; Mersin (İçel); Antakya (ancient Antioch), once one of the greatest cities of the world; and the small but fast-developing fishing ports of Kas and Kalkan.

The popularity of the quiet and lovely village of Kalkan, with its sheltered harbour, is growing each year

THE MEDITERRANEAN COAST

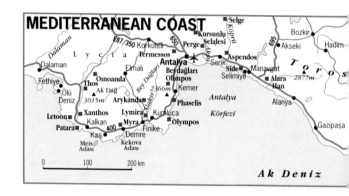

◆◆◆

ALANYA

The lively and popular holiday resort of Alanya is on a delightful stretch of coast on the 'Turkish Riviera', and is sheltered by densely wooded, purple-tinged hills. Two sweeping, sandy bays curve round the headland, where a giant peninsula juts out dramatically into the sea. Known in ancient times as Korakesion, it was founded in the 4th century BC and, during Roman times, was a notorious pirate stronghold. The town was later annexed by Alâeddin Keykubad, becoming his winter residence and his naval base.

From the lower town a road winds round the harbour, with its interesting arched boatyards and medieval octagonal Red Tower, and leads up to the old Seljuk fortress, which keeps watch over Alanya from its impressive rocky perch. The ruins here command superb views across the bay to the distant snow-capped peaks of the Taurus Mountains.

Alanya itself is a labyrinth of shops, bars and restaurants. A

highlight for many visitors is its weekly market, when the stalls spill over with local produce and livestock jostles with the crowd.

Fortress

The well-preserved, double-walled Seljuk fortress of Alanya has 150 towers still standing, and contains mosques, a Byzantine church, a covered bazaar, caravanserai and cisterns. The outer wall is 5 miles (8km) long and took 12 years to build, and some 400 cisterns could store sufficient water to withstand any length of siege. Of particular interest to visitors are a high ceilinged room topped by a vast dome and the remains of the *bedesten* (a domed store), which once boasted 26 rooms and vast storage spaces.

Red Tower

The Red Tower, or Kızıl Kule, which reinforces the low wall of the fortress at the junction of the north and east walls, served as a watchtower, and was built in 1225 after the model of the Crusaders' castles. It has been skilfully restored. The first two storeys are

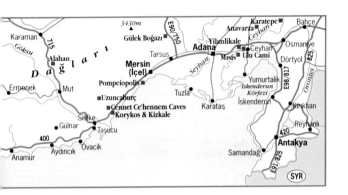

of reddish stone blocks, the two upper ones are built from huge red bricks.

Shipyard
The 13th-century shipyard, whose entrance is flanked by a guardroom on the left and a mosque on the right, consisted of five compartments; its foundations were hewn out of the rock. Turkish warships were built here from timber brought from the Taurus Mountains.

Damlatas Cave
At the foot of the promontory on the eastern side is the Damlatas Cave, thought to be anything up to about 15,000 years old. This boasts wonderful multi-coloured stalagmites and stalactites, and its high humidity is reputed to benefit sufferers from asthma and other respiratory complaints.

Boat Trips
Alanya is one of Turkey's major ports, and the harbour has been extended to accommodate a great number of craft, many of which regularly cruise along the surrounding shores which abound in caves and inlets. Of special interest are the Fosforlu Magara (Blue Grotto), with its phosphorescent rocks, and Kizlar Magarası (Maidens' Cave), where pirates used to keep their female captives.

Sports
Alanya offers good watersports, with waterskiing and windsurfing available at various hotels. There are pedalos and boats for hire, swimming and snorkelling, tennis and table tennis.

Hotels and Restaurants
Alanya boasts numerous international-standard hotels, and many more are under construction. The best, and most expensive, include the **Serapsu**, **Ananas**, **Club Hotel Alantur**, and the **Top Hotel**. Recommended in the medium price bracket are the **Alara**, some distance from the resort, but in a beautiful setting; the **Anilgan**, on the edge of the resort; and the **Boulevard**, right in the centre. The **Atilla** and the **Develi**, also in the heart of things, are popular with those on a budget, as are the **Galaxy** and

the **Sandy**, both some way from the resort.

The resort offers numerous good restaurants serving tasty Turkish specialities, and plenty of bars, cafés and discos. For dancing of a more exotic nature, the hotels' ethnic evenings, with the accent on audience participation, are a good opportunity for some unusual photographs.

Tourism Bureau: Çarsı Mah, Kalearkası Caddesi, Damlatas Yani (tel: 323) 11240). Opposite the museum, near Damlatas Cave.

Excursions from Alanya

The road east of Alanya, through the village of Gazipasa, leads to what is often claimed, and with some justification, to be the most beautiful stretch of coastline in Turkey. The road itself clings to the pine-clad mountain slopes which plunge steeply down to the sea, offering spectacular views of cliffs, coves and the brilliant turquoise waters of the Mediterranean.

Just outside Anamur, 80 miles (128km) from Alanya, are the ruins of ancient Anemurium, with its double ramparts, a theatre, odeon and a necropolis. A fine, well-preserved Crusader castle is nearby, set between curving, sandy beaches, and from the top of the fort there is a splendid view of the countryside and coast. East of Anamur the road rises and falls until you reach the Plain of Silifke. Just before Silifke is the little resort of Tasucu, with its sandy beach and harbour from where regular boat services operate to North Cyprus. Located slightly inland is Silifke itself, 136 miles (217km) beyond

Anamur, set at the foot of a fortress crowning the hill that was the acropolis of ancient Seleucia and Calycadnos. In the town is an old bridge crossing the Calycadnos River, today called the Göksu, and the remains of a Roman theatre, temple and necropolis.

Just beyond Silifke at Narlikuyu is a Roman mosaic depicting the Three Graces. Further on are the deep chasms known as Cennet and Cehennem (Heaven and Hell); Heaven contains the ruins of a 5th-century chapel. Nearby is a deep cave full of stalactites and stalagmites.
End of excursions

♦♦♦
ANTAKYA

Antakya – known as Antioch in ancient times – is pleasantly situated in a fertile plain surrounded by grand mountains and was once the prosperous and ostentatious capital of the Seleucid kings, who were notorious for their indulgent lifestyles. In Roman times the city was a great centre of artistic, scientific and commercial activity. It was also a centre of Christianity, where St Barnabus, St Paul and St Peter all stayed and preached. Traces left by successive occupants of Antioch go back as far as the 4th millennium BC. The town was founded by one of Alexander's generals and was constantly enlarged by subsequent Seleucids, while under the Romans it became the third city of the empire, with 500,000 inhabitants. It was full of theatres, baths, canals and markets, and even had street lighting.

Museum

Most of what has been preserved of the ancient glory is now in the Hatay Archaeological Museum. In addition to items from the various excavations in the surrounding area, it also contains a collection of 2nd- and 3rd-century Roman mosaics, most of which once adorned the luxury villas in the vale 5 miles (8km) to the south. A little outside the town is the Grotto of St Peter, the cave church from which St Peter is said to have preached for the first time and so founded the Christian community.

Valuable items in the Hatay Archaeological Museum on Gunduz Caddesi include this mosaic from a villa in Roman Antioch

◆◆◆
ANTALYA

Antalya is a thriving, increasingly sophisticated town noted for its shady, palm-fringed boulevards, picturesque old quarters and attractive, newly-restored harbour.

The town is splendidly spread over a cliff promontory between the beaches of Konyaaltı and Lara, with mountains forming a dramatic backdrop. Eastward stretches a beautiful length of coastline indented with many streams, with waterfalls cascading down into the sea from the heights of the adjacent cliffs, while the area is further blessed with shady forests, lakes, and one of the world's most pleasant climates.

The town offers a great many diversions for the holiday-maker, as well as being an excellent base for excursions to local beauty spots, and for visits to the ancient sites and spacious beaches in the vicinity.

Founded by Greek settlers in about 1000BC, it was named Attaleia by Attalus II of Pergamon who, foiled in his attempt to take Side, established a naval base here. Known as Satalia to the Crusaders who used the port to avoid Seljuk territory, it was renamed Antalya in the 13th century.

Its principal attractions, which can be visited either on foot or by horse-drawn carriage, include well-preserved city ramparts and the monumental three-arched Hadrian's Gate, in decorated marble, which was built in AD130 to commemorate the emperor's visit to the city. At the edge of the attractive municipal park – a favourite place for promenades amidst a variety of exotic flowers – is the Hıdırlık Kulesi (tower), which was formerly a lighthouse.

Harbour

The narrow winding streets of the old quarter, lined with pretty wooden houses, lead to the bustling harbour, where cruise ships regularly call. Extensively restored and refurbished in recent years, this is now an attractive, lively area with open-air restaurants, terraced bars, souvenir shops and promenades. Declared a conservation area in 1972, the narrow streets of traditional houses leading down to the harbour are enjoying a new lease of life, many as small attractive bars, restaurants, or guesthouses, some displaying locally-made carpets and woven rugs.

Archaeological Museum
On the Konyaaltı Road, at the western edge of the town, is an archaeological museum that houses a rich collection of ceramics, mosaics and figurines found locally. Many of the exhibits are placed outside in a pleasant garden with views across Antalya Bay. An ethnographic section features a display of the nomadic life, with fully furnished tents and photographs of laden camels.

Shopping
The town is also good for shopping, with a colourful market and a wide selection of shops and boutiques, many selling good quality clothing at very reasonable prices.

Beaches
There are two main beaches on either side of Antalya. On the western edge is the huge crescent of the shingle and pebble Konyaaltı Beach, and to the east the long sandy Lara Beach, much the better of the two, and almost a resort in its own right, with several international-standard hotels.

The restored, protected harbour is the focal point of Antalya

Hotels and Restaurants
Antalya is the setting for several of the best hotels in Turkey. The newly-opened luxury **Sheraton Voyager**, is expensive with a huge selection of restaurants, bars and leisure facilities. The 409 rooms and suites provide every possible amenity, from air-conditioning to hairdryers. All rooms have balconies, 80 per cent with sea views. There is also a nightclub, casino, indoor pool, jacuzzi, healthclub, tennis courts, squash court and a children's pool. Also expensive but good are the **Club Sera**, **Antalya Dedeman**, **Falez** and **Ofo**. In the mid-price range are the **Oranj**, the **Altes** and the **Kozan**, and for those on limited budgets the **Aras** and the **Kivrak**. The elegant

Adalya, by the harbour, is also good.
Tourism Bureau: Selçuk Mah, Mermerli Sok, Ahiyusuf Cami Yanı, Kaleiçi (tel: (31) 470541/2).

Excursions from Antalya
Antalya is an excellent base for exploring ancient sites. Southwest takes you through the Bey Dagları (Olympos) National Park to Phaselis, while north is the road to Termessos. To the east are Perge, Aspendos and Side.

PERGE
The ancient site of Perge, which lies 11 miles (18km) east of Antalya, contains much to interest the visitor, not least an impressive theatre and equally impressive stadium. Until the time of Alexander the Great, Perge was an independent city

republic; it then became a principal city of Pamphylia in Hellenistic times. The city prospered under Rome, its importance not declining until the Byzantine period.

Just outside the city walls is a Greco-Roman stadium which could seat 25,000. The colonnaded gallery running round the top was built against a hillside. Adjacent to the stadium is one of the biggest and best-preserved theatres of antiquity, which could seat approximately 15,000.

Through a Roman gate, lies a triumphal arch that has been restored by archaeologists. Further along is the handsome 3rd century BC city gate flanked by two lofty round towers and containing a horseshoe-shaped court. This gate leads on to a long colonnaded way that was once lined with shops and mosaic pavements. Opposite the ruins of the large agora stands a building which used to house the thermal baths and gymnasium.

TERMESSOS
The romantic ruins of the ancient city fortress of Termessos are perched on a craggy peak about 21 miles (34km) from Antalya. In ancient times this mountain area was known as Pisidia, and Termessos was its most powerful city. The ruins are set within a profusion of wild flowers, olive trees and mountain pine, making it one of the most beautiful ancient sites in Turkey.

The city was founded by a war-like, courageous people who put up a successful resistance to Alexander the Great, forcing him to raise his siege and retreat in frustration. He took his revenge by burning the olive groves around the town. Towards the end of the 3rd century AD its fortunes began to decline, and in the 5th century it was abandoned altogether.

The entrance portal to the city is the monumental Hadrian's Gate, through which are traces of a still unexcavated gymnasium and a small theatre which once seated 4,200 people, very few in comparison with the theatres of Pamphylia. The odeon's walls, up to 33ft (10m) in height, still stand and traces of windows are to be seen on the eastern and western walls. To the south of the odeon lies the Temple of Artemis, built in Roman times by the wife of the sculptor who made the temple statue. Next to this, set on a podium, is the Temple of Zeus, the patron god of Termessos. Here reliefs depict a battle between gods and monsters.

◆◆◆
ASPENDOS

Aspendos, just over 30 miles (49km) from Antalya, is also known as Belkis, after the modern village near by. Although it may be said that it was founded as a colony of Argos, it is known to have existed well before. Visitors are immediately confronted with the high outer walls of the theatre, set against the eastern slopes of a small hill and pierced with windows. The high entrance wall impresses, even without the fine works of art which once adorned it. The theatre, from the 2nd century BC, is still used during the annual festival of Antalya, and is capable of seating 15,000 spectators. Apart from the magnificent theatre, other constructions of note on or near the site include the impressive aqueducts and the stadium. The aqueducts have

This bridge in Aspendos is from the time of the Seljuk Turks; some believe the city itself dates from as early as 1180 BC

survived sufficiently in several places to show how superbly designed they were. You can trace these aqueducts by road around the village for ½ mile (0.8km), and on foot from the site by following the footpath around the walls of the acropolis before reaching the stadium, which has a rock tomb to the right and a small sarcophagus to the left.

Waterfalls
Six miles (10km) northeast of Antalya are the spectacular Lower Düden Waterfalls which plunge over the cliff edge to the sea. Further up the same river are the equally spectacular Upper Düden Waterfalls.
End of excursions

KALKAN
Overlooking an attractive harbour, this picturesque fishing village is becoming an increasingly popular resort, thanks to its setting, excellent restaurants and friendly atmosphere. Predominantly a fishing hamlet with a tranquil, sleepy air, it has quaint old houses with wooden balconies overhanging the road. Its narrow streets, some cobbled, house a couple of general stores, a stall selling exotic fruit and vegetables, and a few souvenir shops.

Boats leave the harbour most mornings to ferry visitors to nearby beaches and small bays, although it is possible to swim from jetties down on the small pebbly area on the harbour front. Less than 4 miles (6.4km) east of Kalkan lies Kapitas, a beach of white sand with turquoise waters.

Hotels and Restaurants
The **Patara Prince** is a stylish, 125-bed hotel, fairly expensive by Turkish standards but well worth it. It features a choice of three restaurants, indoor and outdoor swimming pools, a nightclub, floodlit tennis courts and shops. Less expensive recommendations are the **Pirat** and the **Grida Apartotel**, while the **Kalkan Han Pansiyon**, in the centre of the village, has 12 rooms that are much in demand by those with limited funds. There are several pleasant, good value bars and restaurants overlooking the harbour.

Excursions from Kalkan
Popular excursions are to the ancient site of Xanthos, and to Patara, 10 miles (16km) distant, which offers not only one of the finest beaches in Turkey, but also some fascinating ruins (see **Aegean Coast** chapter).
End of excursions

KAS
Nestling at the foot of the Taurus Mountains on the shores of a deep blue bay, this little fishing village has suddenly been 'discovered' by holiday-makers. Its setting is outstanding, encircling a crescent bay at the end of a verdant fjord, enclosed to the north by a long peninsula and sheltered on its seaward side by the lovely Greek islet of Meis Adası (Castellorizo). Kas is one of the oldest settlements in Lycia, though most of the ancient settlement is now covered by the modern village. The rock tombs northeast of the town date from the 4th century BC. On a rise

54

THE MEDITERRANEAN COAST

The beautiful rugs and carpets on sale in Kas make fine souvenirs of Turkey: they are surprisingly reasonable

between the open sea and the hill which was probably the acropolis of Antiphellos, lies a rock tomb in the Doric order, where an inside frieze depicts two dozen dancing female figures. The acropolis was surrounded by a fortified wall, of which traces can be seen on the façade facing the island of Meis Adası (Castellorizo).

To the west of Kas stands the ancient theatre, enjoying a remarkable panorama. Its 26 rows of seats look straight out from the hillside to the sea. Visitors do not come to Kas for the beaches – there are none, apart from a few small stony coves – but for the friendliness of the locals and the natural beauty of this traditional village. Swimming is mainly from rocky

platforms in clear waters, or from the pebbly coves, but you can take a *dolmus* to the sandy beach of Kapitas and the long expanse of sand at Patara is less than 30 miles (48km) away.

Hotels
The **Club Hotel Phellos**, in the heart of the resort, offers 81 rooms, all with private facilities, air-conditioning and balcony. There is a main swimming pool and children's pool, and large outdoor restaurant. The **Kayahan** is cheaper, but also has two pools and a variety of facilities while the simply-furnished and equipped 22-room **Toros** is a popular budget choice.
Tourism Bureau: Cumhuriyet Meydanı 6 (tel: (3226) 1238). On the main square by the harbour.

Excursions from Kas
Excursions are available to Demre, which is associated with the original St Nicholas, or you

can join a boat trip to Kekova, where the sunken ruins of Lycian settlements can be seen.

◆
DEMRE

Some say that the original St Nicholas, or Father Christmas, came not from the wintry lands of snow and igloos but from Turkey. His actual birthplace, in fact, was the village of Patara, but it was at Demre, where a tiny church bears his name, that he served as bishop in the 4th century AD.

Legend has it that when he was young his parents died, leaving him a fortune. Nicholas used the money to help others, especially young people, and girls from families too poor to give them a dowry.

As the St Nicholas cult developed, memory of him faded in his home town, and earlier this century the roofless 5th-century basilica of St Nicholas was used as a substitute for a mosque. With the expansion of tourism, the authorities saw the potential of the building, and after several years of restoration the church was opened in 1981 as a shrine and museum to the saint. Beside the church is a statue of Father Christmas – bearded, robed and trundling a sackful of presents. Every 6th December, the Noel Baba Ceremony attracts many visitors.

◆◆
KEKOVA

The lizard-shaped isle of Kekova, which lies off shore between the ruins of Andriake and Aperlae, is hauntingly beautiful, with Lycian sarcophagi scattered along the shore and lying half-submerged in lovely coves.

End of excursions

KEMER

Tourism first came here when the older yacht marina was built and sailing people started to appear in the town looking for somewhere to eat and buy provisions and souvenirs. Today, the resort's attractive and well designed new marina is attracting even more yachts, giving Kemer an atmosphere not unlike Puerto Banus in Spain, while numerous holiday villages and hotels have also sprung up to satisfy the needs of landlubbers. There are two beaches at the resort. The best is of the sand-mixed-with-pebble variety and stretches round the bay from the marina. The town beach is pebble, with convenient *lokantas* and cafés. The best sandy beach in the area is located on the outskirts, by the Pansiyon Gul 2. Cars can be hired locally, there are plenty of taxis and a good bus service, so getting around is no problem. The regional capital, Antalya, is an hour or so's drive away.

Hotels

Many of the largest and most comprehensive holiday villages in Turkey are here, including two **Club Méditerranée** villages with a combined total of 2,210 beds, both having plenty of facilities and activities. The **Robinson Club**, **Kemer Holiday Club**, **Hydros Village**, **Club Marco Polo**, and **Club Aldiana Milta**, are popular for the same reasons. Of the many new hotels, the unusual **Kiris World Magic** has excellent facilities, including an enormous outdoor pool. Equally good top hotels are the **Phaselis Princess**, **Ramada Renaissance** and **Golden Lotus**.

Recommended mid-price hotels include the **Pegasus Princess** and **Gurkay Beltas**, and for those on a tighter budget, the **Daallar Adonis** and the **Hasan Seker**.

Tourism Bureau: Belediye Binası (tel: (3214) 1536/7). Located near the harbour on the ground floor of the Town Hall.

Excursions from Kemer

PHASELIS

Phaselis is a ten-minute drive away. Here, in beautiful countryside, are the magnificent remains of an ancient city, by the side of an attractive beach. As at Olympos, the setting and atmosphere of Phaselis are very rewarding. The ruins are still being excavated, and although not on the grandest scale, include an attractive walk through a paved market, theatre, aqueduct and temple.

Once a major port with three natural harbours, Phaselis was founded in the 7th century BC as a colony of Rhodes, possibly on an earlier site. It was ruled by the Persians after Darius conquered Anatolia, and later by Alexander the Great, whom the inhabitants admitted without a struggle. After the death of Alexander the city was ruled by the Egyptian Ptolemaic dynasty from 209BC to 197BC, returned to the Rhodians until 160BC and then became part of the Lycian confederacy under Roman rule. The city enjoyed a

great deal of prosperity through all the periods of its history, especially under the Romans. Like Olympos, Phaselis was under constant threat from pirates in the first century BC, and was even ruled for a period by the pirate Zeniketes, until he was defeated by the Romans. During the Byzantine period the city became a bishopric. The vulnerability of its harbours to pirate attack began its decline in the 3rd century AD. By the times the Seljuks conquered the region in the 11th century, Phaselis had ceased to be a port of any note. In the military harbour you can still see the remains of a pier. The ruins in Phaselis are scattered picturesquely among trees that stretch down to the beach. There is a small museum at the entrance.

OLYMPOS

Located between Kemer and the village of Adras, tucked in a rugged mountain gorge on the coast of Lycia, lie the unexcavated, overgrown ruins of this once-great port city. Here, palm trees flourish next to pine trees, citrus fruit is abundant and vegetables are grown year-round. With its mild climate, natural defences and strategic location half-way between Rhodes and Cyprus, it is easy to see why this valley was settled; it is less easy to understand why it was abandoned.

Olympos enjoyed a brief existence during the Hellenistic period, being one of the foremost members of the Lycian confederacy. Coins were struck here in the 2nd century BC, and in

78BC the city became the base of the pirate Zeniketes. He was finally defeated by the Roman governor of Lycia, Publius Servilius Vatia, in a sea battle, and forced to flee. He took refuge in his fortress near Olympos but by accident set his house alight with a torch he carried and was burned to death.

Under Roman rule Olympos became extremely prosperous, since its harbours were ideal for trade, and in AD129, after Hadrian visited the city, it was renamed Hadrianoplois. Opramas, a rich citizen of the Lycian League, paid for the construction of many fine buildings in the 2nd century AD. Towards the end of this century Olympos fell into the hands of pirates once again, and was impoverished as a result. It was used by Venetian and Genoese pirates for a period, during which time the Genoese built a harbour wall. After the pirates were routed by the Ottoman fleet, the city was abandoned altogether. Although small, it is a fascinating site, the ruins of the city being set along the banks of a shallow stream that runs up the middle of the gorge. On the south side of the stream the ancient town wraps above the cliffs overlooking the sea and stretches more than a mile (1.6km) inland. There, among the fallen leaves, marble columns and a small Roman theatre, anonymous intact walls and elevated moss-covered floors fill the flat ground near the stream bed. Roman and Byzantine tombs blanket the steep necropolis on the south side of the ravine.

On the north side of the stream the smooth stone doorway of a

A fine temple doorway, thought to date from the 2nd century bc, may be seen among the jungle of vegetation at Olympos

temple which housed a statue of Marcus Aurelius splits the entangled forest in two. A trail through this doorway leads to roofed Roman baths complete with mosaic floors decorated in bold geometric shapes.

There is, as yet, no modern village nearby, no tourist hotels, no distracting clamour: only an occasional farmer's cottage and a small *pension* a mile (1.6km) down the beach. As part of the Bey Dağları (Olympos) National Park the area is protected from development. Two small winding roads lead down to the site from the high coastal road; the better one comes from Kumluca, through Cavuskoy. The most spectacular approach, however, is by sea from the west. Less than ¼ mile (0.4km) away a wall of mountain blocks the view to the west and a 2 mile (3.2km) expanse of beach backed by lofty Mount Olympos, is visible on the right, but the ruins of Olympos itself are neatly hidden from sight. Not until a final small headland is rounded can one look to the west and see a narrow gorge carved through the mountains. Crumbling walls and towers are just visible above the tree tops on both slopes.

In its golden age the port must have been full of ships, the streets full of people, and the steep hillsides full of stately buildings.

End of excursions

MERSIN (IÇEL)

With its shady, palm-lined avenues, city park and modern hotels, set amidst lush market gardens, Mersin (or, Içel) is an attractive and convenient base from which to visit nearby historical sites and the many beaches and coves in the vicinity. The largest port on the Turkish Mediterranean, with a regular car ferry service to North Cyprus. Mersin is a rapidly developing city, with an attractive waterfront. The old part of town contains numerous shops and reasonably-priced restaurants.

Hotels

The **Hilton** offers the type of standards and facilities generally associated with this chain. A good mid-price range hotel is the **Club Soli**, about 6 miles (10km) from the city centre, and for those on a budget the **Ezgi Hotel** is recommended.

Tourism Bureau: Ismet Inönü Bulv 5/1, Liman Girisı (tel: (74) 312710).

Excursion from Mersin

TARSUS

About half-an-hour's drive from Mersin (Içel) is Tarsus, renowned as the birthplace of the Apostle St Paul. It is also the place where Cleopatra had her first meeting with Mark Antony.

End of excursion

SIDE

An ancient fishing village situated about 50 miles (80km) east of Antalya and surrounded by fertile green plains, Side is developing into one of Turkey's premier holiday resorts.

Side's popularity is based on the resort's beautiful beaches, fascinating classical ruins and its friendly, informal atmosphere. The colourful main thoroughfare, now filled with an array of craft shops, bars and restaurants, follows the route of the original Roman colonnaded street. At one end are the well-preserved amphitheatre and the old Roman baths, which now house the impressive Side Museum.

The exact date of Side's foundation is not clear, although it is thought it was established in the 7th century BC as a colony of the Aeolian city of Cyme. The city really began to flourish in the 2nd century BC, when it was the principal port in the region for the landing of slaves taken by the corsairs. The pirates were finally

Cleopatra is supposed to have bathed in the sea at Side, after an assignation with Mark Antony

crushed in 67BC, so ending Side's prosperity.

It flourished again in the 2nd century AD, when much of its income was used to adorn the city with magnificent buildings; it is the remains of these which have survived. As Rome's power declined, so too did Side's importance, though it flourished once again in early Byzantine times, only to decline finally with the Arab invasions in the middle of the 7th century. It was eventually destroyed by fire in the 10th century. For the next thousand years it was left deserted.

Roman Agora

Among the many ruins are those of the immense Roman agora, built in the 2nd century BC and consisting of the usual porticoed court lined with vaulted shops.

The ruins of a round structure at the centre of the agora are believed to be those of a Temple of Tyche, the goddess of fortune.

Roman Baths (Side Museum)

Directly across from the agora are the Roman baths, which have been superbly restored and now house a delightful museum exhibiting some of the finest Roman statues in Asia Minor, all of them discovered on the site in recent years.

Roman Theatre

Just beyond the agora is the Roman theatre, the most impressive monument in Side. This was built in the 2nd century AD, and is similar to that at Aspendos. In later Roman times the orchestra was used for the performance of gladiatorial combats, and in the 5th century two open-air Christian sanctuaries were constructed there, with the congregation seated in the auditorium. There is an excellent panorama from the upper tier of the theatre.

Inner Walls
The theatre formed part of the inner wall of the city, built in the 4th century AD, and the main gate leads to the ruins of a late Roman temple of Dionysus. From there the road out towards the end of the peninsula follows the route of an ancient colonnaded street.

Harbour
At the south side of the ancient harbour, now almost completely silted up, are the remains of two adjoining temples, one dedicated to Athena and the other to Apollo. Behind these is a Byzantine basilica, and nearby is a temple dedicated to Man, the Anatolian God of the Moon.

Sports
Side offers good watersports facilities including windsurfing, waterskiing and sailing, as well as swimming and snorkelling. Many hotels also have tennis and table tennis facilities.

Hotels
There is now an enormous range of hotels, with the **Asteria**, **Cesars Hotels and Casino**, and the **Novotel** among the best at the top of the range; and the **Sirma** and **Defne** in the medium/lower price category. Of the many holiday villages, the **Robinson Club** has an excellent range of sports facilities.
Tourism Bureau: Side Yolu Üzeri (tel: (321) 31265 & 32657). Located at the entrance crossroads into Side.

Excursions from Side
Side's historical ruins are among the best in the area and provide a fascinating insight into Turkey's past. There are also several other well-preserved sites worth exploring in the vicinity, at Perge, Aspendos and Termessos. Alternatively, take a leisurely cruise on the Manavgat River to the Manavgat Falls, where kingfishers and terrapins dive among the reeds, or go shopping in Alanya or Antalya.
End of excursions

HOW TO GET TO THE MEDITERRANEAN COAST

By Air
Regular scheduled and charter flights operate from many international airports to Antalya, but tend to be less frequent in the winter. It is also possible to fly to Istanbul or Ankara and take a connecting flight to Antalya. Coach and taxi services are available from Antalya airport to the centre of town.
Approximate distances by road from Antalya to the principal Turkish Mediterranean holiday resorts are: Kemer 26 miles (42km), Side 46½ miles (75km), Alanya 84 miles (135km). Some of the Mediterranean resorts are more easily accessible from Dalaman Airport, such as Kas, which is 98 miles (158km) from Dalaman; others, such as Antakya and Mersin (Içel), are closer to Adana Airport.

By Boat
Frequent services and cruises sail to the principal ports on the Mediterranean coast. Turkish Maritime Lines also operate summer services from Istanbul and Izmir to Fethiye, Kas, Finike, Antalya, Alanya and Mersin (Içel).

CENTRAL TURKEY

Central Turkey is home to one of the country's most impressive natural wonders: the amazing region of ancient Cappadocia, with its awe-inspiring rock cones, canyons, churches, capped pinnacles and underground cities. Visits to Cappadocia are extensively featured by tour companies, either as an integral part of a coach tour of the country, or as organised excursions from the premier Aegean and Mediterranean holiday resorts, and the region is also attracting increasing numbers of visitors on fly/drive packages.

Ankara, Turkey's capital, is also located in the country's heartland, which is officially known as Central Anatolia, as is the city of Konya, one of Turkey's oldest continuously inhabited sites and home of the Mevlevi sect, internationally known as the Whirling Dervishes.

Slashed by ravines and dotted with volcanic peaks, the Central Anatolian plateau – one of the cradles of civilisation – is covered with wheat fields and lines of poplars in the valleys. In its turbulent history the region has seen the march of such invaders as Alexander the Great and Tamerlane, and everywhere is evidence of the various influences that have been at work, from the Christian frescoes in the rock churches of Cappadocia's Göreme valley, to Seljuk architecture in Konya.

The remarkable lunar landscape of the Göreme valley, Cappadocia, was formed through volcanic activity

CENTRAL TURKEY

◆◆◆
ANKARA

On a hill overlooking the Turkish capital of Ankara is an imposing monument to the man without whom this land of dramatic physical contrasts would have been reduced to little more than a patch of steppeland: General Mustafa Kemal. It was he who roused a people already exhausted by the Ottoman defeat in World War I, drove the invading forces into the sea, and won back for the Turks their homeland. Given the name Atatürk ('Father of the Turks'), Mustafa Kemal founded the Turkish Republic in 1923 and became its first president. Anxious to distance himself and his Republic from the Ottoman years, he decided to shift the capital from Istanbul and create a brand new one on the Anatolian plains, basing it on what was then a small town with a population of about 75,000.

Today, Ankara has a population of over three million, and is growing fast.

Though the city is thoroughly modern in appearance, there were settlements on this spot as far back as 1500BC, the town's fortunes being governed by its position near the centre of the vast Anatolian plateau, making it a prosperous stopping-off point on major trade routes. In the 8th century BC the Phrygians established the city of Ancyra on the site, and five centuries later the Galatians made Ancyra their capital.

Modern Ankara has few remaining vestiges of its past, and in most respects is much less interesting to the visitor than Istanbul. Nevertheless, interspersed among the many modern office buildings and shops is evidence of its not-forgotten past: an ancient citadel, Roman baths and Ottoman mosques.

One aspect of Ankara that takes many visitors by surprise, and pleasantly so, is the city's greenery. Atatürk loved trees and had them planted practically everywhere, surrounding the city with a delightful green belt in spite of the area's intrinsically harsh terrain. And on the outskirts he built a model farm where, today, Ankara residents and visitors go to enjoy the scenery and the fresh air.

Citadel

Ankara's citadel dominates the top of a rocky summit. Its inner section was built in the 7th century when Arab invasions were particularly frequent in Asia Minor. In the 9th century Mihail II had a second wall built round the first to help fortify the citadel against invasion. This outer wall surrounds the fortress in the shape of a heart.

In its long history the citadel had been captured and damaged a number of times, yet 15 towers are still standing. Although the actual form of these walls dates from Byzantine and Seljuk times, the building material, such as marble, came from the Romans. Within the castle is a warren of narrow lanes flanked by numerous 17th- and 18th-century wooden houses, where life goes on much as it has for centuries.

Temple of Augustus

This was originally built in the 2nd century BC, and was first

Ankara is the embodiment of 20th-century Turkey, but the occasional maze of narrow cobbled streets survives

dedicated to Cybele, the mother goddess of the Anatolians, then to the Phrygian god of the moon; and finally to the Emperor Augustus. In the 5th century AD, after various alterations, it was converted into a Byzantine church.

Roman Baths

Located to the west of the Temple of Augustus, these 3rd-century baths were built by the Emperor Caracalla and dedicated to Asclepios, god of health. They were destroyed by fire in the 10th century, but remain fine examples of Roman architecture, notable for their column-adorned passage, vast dimensions and the impressive pathway to the gymnasium.

Museum of Anatolian Civilisations

Housed in two 15th-century covered bazaar buildings, skilfully combined, is one of the most impressive museums in Turkey: a treasure-house of archaeological finds, including the finest collection of Hittite art and craft in the world. Beautiful pottery, finely-worked gold jewellery and miniature statuary are among the most impressive exhibits. (Closed Mondays).

Atatürk Mausoleum

Begun in 1944 and completed in 1953, this mausoleum to the man who, more than anyone else, brought Turkey into the 20th century, stands 69ft (21m) high and was built in the classical style. It has a porch with a monumental staircase (33 steps in all) decorated with bas reliefs. The Tower of Liberty stands to the right of this staircase; the Tower of Independence to the left. Before the stairway is an imposing paved esplanade lined with galleries and museums, its towers symbolising the Republic, the Revolution, Victory and Peace. A magnificent processional avenue, flanked by cypress trees and 12 Hittite lions, ends at the esplanade.

The inscription on the mausoleum is part of Atatürk's 'The Testament to Youth'. The mausoleum was designed in the form of a temple, surrounded by porticos with quadrangular pillars of fine limestone. The walls of the main chamber are faced with red-veined marble, and the ceiling is sumptuously decorated with golden mosaics of Turkish motifs. The bronze doors were made in Italy and the tomb itself is a single block of marble weighing 40 tons (40.6 tonnes). There is also a museum (closed Monday) containing personal items and a history of the founding of the republic. The mausoleum (open daily) is situated in the Anıttepe quarter.

Atatürk's House

In Cankaya, in the grounds of the Presidential Palace, Atatürk's House remains much as it was in Atatürk's time, and is now a museum. (Open afternoons: Sundays and public and religious holidays).

Column of Julian

The Column of Julian, which stands 49ft (15m) high, is thought to have been erected towards the end of the 4th century to commemorate the visit of the Roman Emperor Julian to the city. Composed of fluted stones, it has a capital decorated with acanthus ornaments.

Hacı Bayram Mosque

Built in the first half of the 15th century, this mosque was decorated by the well-known artist Mustafa towards the end of the 17th century and ornamented with Kütahya tiles in the early 18th century. The Tomb of Hacı Bayram Veli is adjacent.

Hotels and Restaurants

There is a good range of hotels in all price brackets.
Recommended at the upper end of the scale are the new **Ankara Sheraton Hotel & Towers**, with 342 rooms and a wealth of facilities; the 327-room **Ankara Hilton**; the **Merit Altinel**; and the longer-established **Büyük Ankara**. Slightly cheaper is the **Ankara Dedeman**, also with good amenities, and for those on a budget the **Elit** and the **Çevikoglu** are recommended. Among the many restaurants, the **Liman**, and the more expensive **R.V.**, in the Embassy quarter, are recommended.
Tourism Bureau: Gazi Mustafa Kemal Bulvarı 33, Demirtepe (tel: (4) 2317380 and 2317395). In Ankara: freephone 900447090.

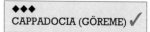

◆◆◆
CAPPADOCIA (GÖREME) ✓

The story of Cappadocia begins about three million years ago, when the volcanoes of Erciyes and Hasan erupted time after time, covering the Central Anatolian plateau with a thick layer of lava and volcanic ash. As the violent upheavals diminished, rain, snow, wind and extremes of

In Cappadocia life continues much as it has always done; tourism is an unknown new ingredient

temperature eroded and sculpted the volcanic rock into the surrealist landscape we see today. The shape of the hard basalt far beneath also played its part, by resisting the erosion to which the malleable volcanic rock submitted so willingly. Described by the Turkish tourism authorities as 'fairy chimneys', the rocky outcrops in Cappadocia's Zelve valley in particular vary in colour from ash grey to beige, yellow, rust and brick red, depending on the time of day. At sunset, as the last light of the sun slips away, combinations of navy blue, lilac, green, pale pink and gold highlights change constantly until they make way for the mysterious silvery shadows of the moonlight.

Cappadocia abounds in myths and legends about giants, fairies and genies, originating in the days when men had no explanation for this extraordinary landscape. It needs little imagination to see the terrain peopled with dervishes, giants and other figures turned to stone: the guardians of a natural wonderland.

History

From the third millennium BC there were small city states in the area, and during the Hattian, Proto-Hattian and Hittite periods the region gained strategic importance due to its position on the trade route to Persia. With the fall of the Hittite Empire in the 12th century BC, the Anatolian dark ages began. Little is known about this period, but the dark ages can be said to have ended when the Lydians gained domination of Anatolia at the beginning of the 6th century BC. In 334BC Anatolia was conquered by Alexander the Great, and until AD17, when the region became a province of the Roman Empire, life here went its relatively peaceful way under the rule of local dynasties.

Neither the Romans nor the Byzantines made any effort to assimilate Anatolia into their own cultures. They were concerned with it only for its strategic trade location, and a source of manpower for their armies. From the east, across Anatolia, came cotton, lemons, melons, sesame, figs, ducks and other commodities. While the Romans founded cities along this trade route through Central Anatolia, the local people preferred the rocky valleys of Cappadocia,

CENTRAL TURKEY

usually hollowing their houses out of the soft rock. For heat insulation, these rock homes match up to the best modern technology, and still today the local inhabitants are waging a struggle to be allowed to go on living in their traditional homes. Throughout the ages Cappadocia has been not only a trade crossroads but also a cultural melting pot where different philosophies, cultures and religions mingled and interacted. When St Paul passed through Cappadocia in the first century he observed that the people worshipped such diverse gods as Zeus, Mitra, Attis and Dionysus, and the new doctrines of Christianity had to put forward convincing arguments against all these pagan beliefs in order to supplant them. Yet it was here that the early Christians, fleeing first from Roman and later from Arab persecution, took refuge and built their churches, monasteries and underground cities in the rock.

The tiny picturesque churches hollowed out of the cliffs were painted and adorned with frescos, in which recurring figures include Anastasius, Gregory, John Chrisostomus and Basil of Caesarea. Basil stands out from the others for his extensive culture, tolerance, knowledge and enlightened teaching, and was known as the 'Pillar of Truth' and 'Interpreter of the Heavens'. By the time the Seljuk Turks entered Cappadocia in the second half of the 11th century, over one thousand sects existed there. Such amicable relations were established between the Christians of Cappadocia and the

In the village of Ürgüp, with its enormous cliff of volcanic rock, houses are often built adjoining the rock pyramids

Seljuks that pictures of Seljuk sultans shared the walls with Orthodox saints. Like the Roman and Byzantine conquerors before them, the Seljuks were more concerned with their economies than anything else, and all along the trade route known as the Sultan's Road passing through Konya, Kayseri and Sivas, they built caravanserais and mosques, many of which are still standing. In the mid-13th century the Moghul invasions brought the Seljuk Empire tumbling, and Anatolia was divided into a number of principalities, of which Karamanoglu, the most powerful, ruled until the Ottoman Empire won control of the region in the

14th century. Under the Turkish-Greek Population Exchange Agreement of the 1920s, nearly all the Greek Orthodox community of Cappadocia migrated to Greece.
Today, the ancient region of Cappadocia is known as Göreme, and is part of the area forming Göreme National Park.

What to see in Cappadocia (Göreme)

Aksaray

A journey east across the vast Konya plain takes us to the beautiful Sultan Han Caravanserai, 25 miles (40km) west of Aksaray. Built in 1229 during the reign of the Seljuk Sultan Keykubat I, this magnificent building features the carved stone portal so characteristic of Seljuk architecture, watchtowers, high walls for defence, a small mosque, a kitchen, bedrooms, workshops, baths and stables.

Out on the monotonous steppe landscape, Aksaray – with its poplars, pines, willows and fruit orchards – emerges into view like an oasis. An important halt on the trade route throughout history, Aksaray was founded by the Hittites, but its remaining monuments all date from the Seljuk and Karamanoglu periods.

Ihlara Valley

Almost 7 miles (11km) from Aksaray, a side road branches off to the right, through typical Cappadocian villages that give one the impression of being cut off completely from the outside world, to the valley of Ihlara. Through this sheer-sided valley, 6 miles (10km) long, flows the Melendiz River, which carries the perpetually melting snows of Mount Hasan and is bordered by poplars, cypresses and pistachio trees. A total of 435 steps follow a steep winding path into the valley, in whose depths are around 100 rock churches and innumerable rock houses.

Underground Cities

The Nigde road south of Nevsehir takes you to two of the underground cities in the area: Kaymaklı and Derinkuyu. Although used subsequently by Christians fleeing persecution, they are pre-Christian in origin, and consist of a labyrinth of underground tunnels and chambers forming numerous storeys. The upper storeys were used as a church and living quarters, while the lower storeys consisted of storage rooms. The labyrinths were designed in such a way that even if the main

CENTRAL TURKEY

entrance were discovered it would be impossible to find the way to the shelters. Moreover, upright grinding stones were placed ready to block the entrances at a moment's notice. Descending to a total depth of 131ft (40m), the underground cities were linked by tunnels, and supplied with a steady stream of fresh air via efficient ventilation systems. Guides with a fairly good command of several languages are usually readily available to show you round.

Göreme Valley
Within Göreme National Park, 5 miles (8km) northwest of Ürgüp, the **Göreme Open-Air Museum**

A rock house in Göreme, complete with precarious outside ladder linking the different levels

(open 08.30–17.00hrs) consists of numerous rock churches with wonderful frescoes. Most of the chapels date from the 10th and 11th centuries. Among the most visited are the Elmalı Kilise (Church with an Apple), the smallest and most recent of the group; the Karanlık Kilise (Dark Church), with its fine paintings and table and benches carved from the rock; the Çarıklı Kilise (Church with Sandals), so called because of the two footprints under the fresco of the Ascension; and the Yılanlı Kilise (Church with Snakes), which has fascinating frescos of the damned in the coils of serpents. On the road to Avcılar, is the Tokalı Kilise (Church with a Buckle), decorated with very fine 10th-century New Testament scenes. Scattered around the valley are many interesting but less accessible churches, while on the road leading north are the troglodyte village of Avcılar, with its houses attached to rock cones; Çavusin, with churches in a rock face; the red-coned monastic complex of Zelve; and Avanos, famous for its pottery and onyx.

Ürgüp
About 6 miles (10km) from Göreme is Ürgüp, the oldest settlement in the area, set against an enormous cliff of volcanic rock, where the pinnacles of rock are as impressive as they are plain.

Hotels
Most of the hotels serving visitors to Cappadocia are in either Nevsehir or Ürgüp. Among those recommended in the former are the impressive **Nevsehir Dedeman**, with 350 rooms and excellent facilities and, in the

The interior of the Alaeddin Mosque in Konya, built in 1220; the columns that support the ceiling were taken from an ancient Graeco-Roman site

mid-price category, the **Altinöz**, **Sehir Palas**, and **Sekeryapan**. The 25-room **Sems** is popular with those on a budget. About 4½ miles (7km) from Nevsehir lies the **Club Méditerranée Kaya Hotel** with 70 rooms, pool, children's pool and nightclub. In Ürgüp, the **Dinler**, **Mustafa** and **Perissia** are all good. Cheaper is the **Cappadocia Merit** holiday village, half a mile (0.8km) from the city centre. The **Basak Palas** and **Bey** are good budget options. **Tourism Bureaux**: Atatürk Caddesi, Hastane Yanı, Nevsehir (tel: (485) 11137, 12712 & 13659); Kayseri Caddesi 37,Ürgüp (tel: (4868) 1059).

◆◆
KONYA
At the heart of the Anatolian plateau 160 miles (260km) south of Ankara, Konya attracts visitors for two main reasons: its beautiful Seljuk architecture; and the mausoleum of the poet, scholar, mystic and philosopher Mevlâna Celâleddin Rumi (1207-73), founder of the sect known throughout the world as the Whirling Dervishes. According to the Phrygian legend, Konya was the first city to emerge after the Flood. There were prehistoric and Hittite settlements there, but the first important town was founded by the Phrygians.
It was in the 12th century that the Konya Plain experienced its second cultural renaissance when the city became the capital of the Seljuk Turks. Migrating from the steppes of Central Asia, the Seljuks served the Byzantines a crushing defeat in 1071 at Malazgirt, which opened the floodgates to the Turkish settlement of Anatolia. Under the enlightened rule of the Sultan Alâeddin Keykubad, Seljuk culture reached its zenith in 13th-century Konya. It was in this environment that one of the Moslem mystic movements was born.

Mevlâna's doctrine was the seeking after good in all its positive manifestations, together with the practice of infinite tolerance. He condemned slavery and advocated monogamy. As the symbol of the shedding of earthly ties, he devised the whirling dance, accompanied by the ethereal sound of the reed flute, which can still be seen each December, during the Mevlâna Festival.

Mevlâna Mausoleum

Housed in the old monastery where the Order of Dervishes was found, this is the city's best known landmark. Dominated by a conical turquoise-blue dome, it contains a remarkable museum of Islamic art, as well as Rumi's sarcophagus. Of special interest are the earliest manuscript of Mevlâna's great mystic epic poem, *The Mesnevi*, and some of the few surviving illuminated manuscripts, as well as early musical instruments, Dervish garments, carpets, silks, fine prayer rugs, and a mass of finely crafted religious artefacts. (Closed Monday).

Alâeddin Mosque

Completed during the reign of Alâeddin Keykubad, this mosque is in the Syrian style, unusual for Anatolia, with a wooden ceiling instead of a high dome, and simple, unadorned brick arches supported by 42 columns. The pulpit and altar are masterpieces of wood-carving.

Karatay Medresesi

Now housing the Museum of Ceramic Art, containing lovely displays of rare Seljuk ceramics, this was built in the 13th century.

The interior of the building is itself a riot of beautiful blue tiles. (Closed Monday).

Hotels

Of the numerous hotels and *pensions* in Konya, the **Özkaymak Park** and the **Selçuk** are two of the best.

Tourism Bureau: Mevlâna Caddesi 22 (tel: (33) 511074). Near the Mevlâna Mausoleum.

HOW TO GET TO CENTRAL TURKEY

By Air

Ankara (Esenboga) Airport is well served by scheduled flights from major international cities. In addition, numerous domestic flights connect Ankara with Turkey's regional airports.

By Road

Ankara is also well served by bus services, approximate road distances being: Istanbul 282 miles (454km), Izmir 362 miles (582km), Konya 160 miles (258km), Cappadocia 174 miles (280km). The E5 road from Istanbul is the busiest highway in Turkey; delays are frequent.

By Rail

Between Istanbul and Ankara there are frequent day and night express services, and between Ankara and Kayseri there is also a regular express service. Car-trains operate from Istanbul to Konya. The Istanbul–Ankara Blue Train (Mavi Tren) takes about 8¼ hours; the Anatolia Express night train has sleeping cars. A faster service is the Istanbul–Ankara Fatih Express departing at 10.30hrs daily. From Izmir there are regular express trains to Ankara, taking about 15 hours.

ISTANBUL

Istanbul is one of the world's most fascinating and exciting cities. Its intriguing blend of old and new, East and West, combined with its strategic setting bridging the continents of Europe and Asia, make a visit here unforgettable. As former capital of three world empires, Istanbul's contrasts are apparent everywhere, from the sirens of the ships to the timeless sounds of muezzins calling the faithful to prayer; from the sunlight flashing off the golden crescent of the mosque domes to the hypnotic gaze of Byzantine mosaic figures. But Istanbul is not just historic – it is still a great city, vividly alive. Beneath the little-changing skyline of its domes and minarets there is the continual bustle and movement of the crowd; the rumbling of vehicles along the ancient cobbled streets; the incessant coming and going of the ferries; and the cries of street-sellers mingling with the sounds of shipping in the busy port.

The old city is set on a triangular promontory between the Golden Horn and the Sea or Marmara, and is defended on the landward side by its massive Byzantine walls, now being painstakingly restored, and declared by UNESCO a World Cultural Heritage site. Here the Emperor Justinian built Christendom's greatest church, St Sophia, now a museum.

Facing St Sophia is the elegant mosque of Sultan Ahmet I, better known as the Blue Mosque because of its magnificent internal decoration of blue Iznik tiles..

There are superb views across the Bosphorus from the top of Topkapı Palace, Istanbul

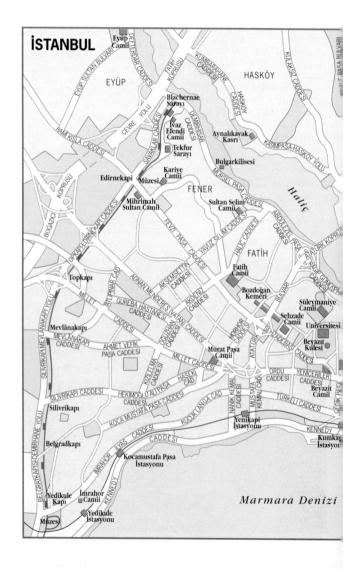

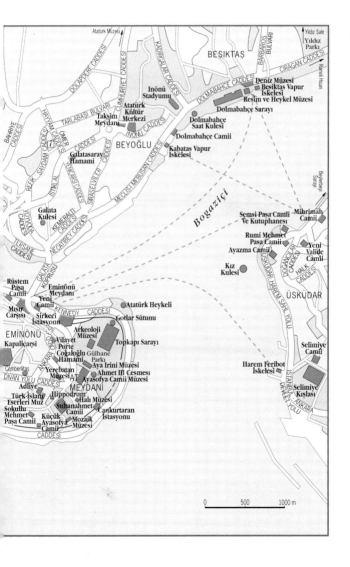

ISTANBUL AND SURROUNDINGS

Another of Istanbul's most magical tourist sights is Topkapı Palace, former residence of the Ottoman rulers and now an irresistible museum housing a wealth of treasures.

A visit to Istanbul's world-famous Covered Bazaar, with its staggering collection of 4,000 shops, is also high on most visitors' list of priorities, if only to soak up the wonderful Oriental atmosphere. Shopping, indeed, is one of the many delights of a visit to Istanbul, and as well as the unique appeal of the Covered Bazaar, the city's modern streets contain boutiques selling up-to-the-minute fashions, while just about everywhere you will encounter the more traditional shops selling items of silver, gold, leather and all manner of hand-crafted articles.

During the past few years a major programme of reconstruction and restoration work has started to beautify the city and to preserve many of its most important quarters, buildings and monuments.

In the recent past, for instance, the famous Golden Horn had become heavily polluted by industrial waste from nearby factories. Now, these factories have been demolished and the banks of the inlet turned into green parks. Meanwhile, water pipes along the bank carry sewage off to the depths of the Marmara Sea. The construction of the Galata Bridge spanning the Golden Horn at its mouth and connecting major commercial districts on both banks is a major step in speeding up the flow of traffic in the densely populated areas of the city, while at Aksaray the first section of a long-awaited metro system has been completed.

Another major undertaking is the restoration of the ancient land walls of the city, spanning the west side of the peninsula and connecting the sea walls along the Golden Horn in the north and those along the Sea of Marmara in the south. After the restoration, many of the moats outside the walls will be filled with water, and other plans call for the building of open-air theatres, parks and sports facilities.

The Turkish Touring and Automobile Association has also been playing a major role in Istanbul's beautification, having restored and converted several old mansions into stylish hotels, and restored and opened up to the public numerous attractive tea houses and restaurants in the city's many parks.

These, and many other improvements schemes taking place throughout Istanbul, are adding considerably to the city's attractions, making a visit here of even a week too short a time to soak up its atmosphere and savour its splendours: the ancient churches, mosques, palaces, bazaars and restaurants, coffee shops and tea houses, delightful parks, and exotic nightlife, not to mention fascinating excursions along the Bosphorus, with perhaps a delicious freshly-caught seafood lunch on one of the surrounding islands.

Istanbul has an exotic style all of its own, which cannot compare with any other city (or capital) in Europe.

*The Harem in Topkapı evokes many
a colourful tale*

What to see in Istanbul

Palaces

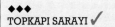

♦♦♦
TOPKAPI SARAYI ✓

No visit to Istanbul would be
complete without a trip to the
amazing Topkapı Palace, former
residence of the Ottoman rulers
and now a museum housing a
wealth of treasures, including a
priceless collection of Chinese
porcelain, a display of famous
jewels from the Imperial Treasury,
and an exhibition of the robes worn
by the sultans and their families.
The jewels of the Treasury are
particularly impressive: an
Aladdin's cave overspilling into
four rooms. The breathtaking
effect is enhanced by the display
of turban crests, jewel-studded
armour and helmets, every
possible utensil and weapon
encrusted with diamonds and
pearls, and no fewer than three
thrones. The famous emerald
dagger, star of the film *Topkapi*,
is outshone by the 86-carat
Spoonmaker diamond.
Beside the imposing gate to the
palace is the elegant fountain of
Sultan Ahmet III. In the first court
stands the ancient Church of St
Irene, one of the oldest Christian
churches in Istanbul, and on the
left of the second court, shaded
by cypresses and plane trees, is
the palace kitchen, now housing
an exquisite collection of silver,
crystal and Chinese porcelain.
The Harem, entered through a
gate on the right side of the court,
was the secluded quarters of the
wives and concubines of the
sultan. In the third court is the
Audience Hall of the sultan, then
the Library of Ahmet III. This
leads to an exhibition of robes
worn by the sultans and their
families, the jewel display, and
finally an exhibition of miniatures.
In the fourth court is the Pavilion

of the Holy Mantle, enshrining relics of the Prophet Mohammed. (Closed Tuesday).

◆◆◆
DOLMABAHÇE SARAYI

Built in the mid-19th century by Sultan Abdülmecit, the palace has a huge frontage on to the Bosphorus. Particularly impressive is the vast reception salon supported by 56 columns, containing a huge crystal chandelier. Also of special interest are the Harem and the Bird Pavilion. (Closed Monday and Thursday).

◆◆
BEYLERBEYI SARAYI

Located on the Asian side of the Bosphorus, this palace was built by Sultan Abdülaziz in 1865 of white marble, and has a beautiful garden with magnolia trees. It was used as a summer residence of the sultans and a guesthouse for visiting foreign dignitaries. (Closed Monday and Thursday).

◆◆
YILDIZ SARAYI

This is a complex of pavilions, a palace and a mosque built over a long period of time and by several sultans but completed by Abdülhamit II at the end of the 19th century. The Sale, largest and most splendid of the buildings, reflects the luxurious lifestyle of the period. The palace is set in a large park situated on the crest of a hill, offering panoramic views.
Only the Sale and park are accessible as restoration work is in progress. (Sale: closed Monday and Thursday. Park: open daily).

Museums

◆◆◆
ST SOPHIA (AYASOFYA CAMII MÜZESI) ✔

The present St Sophia is the third building with this name to occupy the same site. The first church was completed in 360 in the reign of Constantius, son of Constantine the Great. This church was destroyed by fire in 404. Theodosius II's new church was dedicated in 415, but this, too, was destroyed by fire in 532. Emperor Justinian began work on the present basilica in 532 and it was completed in 537. Designed by Anthemius and the architect Isidorus, the building immediately earned far-reaching admiration both for its dome and

St Sophia became a mosque in the 16th century

for its dazzling ornamentation. The basilica underwent repairs in 994. Later it was looted by European Christians who came to Istanbul with the army of the Fourth Crusade. According to accounts of Russian priests who visited Istanbul in the 15th century, St Sophia was in a virtually abandoned state at the period. In 1453, with the conquest of Istanbul by the Turks, the building was taken over and reorganised. Remains from such ancient cities as Sheba, Ephesus and Baalbek were used in the building's reconstruction and the original walls of St Sophia were decorated with coloured marble and mosaics.

Inside, above the south door is a striking mosaic depicting Mary sitting on a throne, with the Infant Jesus on her lap and two figures to her left and right. The figure on the left is Constantine the Great,

presenting to Mary the city which he founded; and on the right is St Justinian, offering a model of St Sophia. Above the main door, the Emperor's Gate, is a mosaic portraying Jesus, Mary and the Angel Gabriel. Rampways on four sides of the building lead to the upper galleries. The western side of the top-floor galleries was reserved for the Empress and for the wives of the leading members of the state. In the south gallery there is a section known as the Consul's Meeting Hall. In the middle of the right-hand wall of the hall is a mosaic portraying Jesus, Mary and John the Baptist, whilst on the east wall are depicted the Emperor Constantine and the Empress Zoe offering to an enthroned Jesus a purse of gold and the imperial edict which ordered the creation of the city.

The Ayasofya café is located in a corner of the museum's shady garden. (Museum closed Monday).

◆◆
KARIYE CAMII

The 11th-century St Saviour in Chora (meaning, 'in the country') is, after St Sophia, the most important Byzantine monument in Istanbul. The walls are decorated with superb 14th-century frescoes and mosaics on a gold background. The church is a remarkable museum of Byzantine art, and has a quiet garden with a café. (Closed Tuesday).

◆◆
ST IRENE (AYA IRINI MÜZESI)

St Irene was the first church in Istanbul, built by Constantine in the 4th century and rebuilt by Justinian. It is reputedly the site of a pre-Christian temple. (Closed Monday).

ARCHAEOLOGICAL MUSEUMS (ARKEOLOJI MÜZESI)
These are situated at the boundary of the first court of the Topkapı Palace. The rich collection of antiquities in the **Archaeological Museum** includes the celebrated Alexander Sarcophagus, while the **Museum of the Ancient Orient** displays antiquities from the Hatti, Hittite, Assyrian, Babylonian and Sumerian civilisations. (Closed Monday).

MUSEUM OF TURKISH CERAMICS (CINILI KÖSK)
A pavilion built by Sultan Mehmet II in the 15th century, displays beautiful Iznik tiles from the 16th century and fine Seljuk and Ottoman examples. (Closed Monday).

MUSEUM OF TURKISH ART (TÜRK ISLAM ESERLERI MÜZESI)
Built in 1524 the Palace of Ibrahim Pasa was the grandest private residence ever constructed in the Ottoman Empire. It is now a museum with many Turkish and Persian miniatures, Seljuk tiles and antique carpets. (Closed Monday).

NAVAL MUSEUM (DENIZ MÜZESI)
Located in the Besiktas neighbourhood, this museum contains the great imperial caiques that were used to row the sultans across the Bosphorus, as well as many interesting exhibits from Ottoman naval history. (Closed Monday and Tuesday).

MILITARY MUSEUM (ASKERI MÜZESI)
The exhibits from Ottoman history on show here include the great field tents used on campaigns. Ottoman military bands play each afternoon. (Closed Monday and Tuesday).

ATATÜRK MÜZESI
The house where Atatürk lived in Sisli contains his personal effects. (Closed weekends).

SADBERK HANIM MÜZESI
A charming museum dedicated to old Turkish arts and handicrafts, also with an archaeological section, situated on the Bosphorus at Büyükdere. (Closed Wednesday).

MUSEUM OF FINE ARTS (RESIM VE HEYKEL MÜZESI)
Located at Besiktas, this is widely considered one of the finest museums in Turkey, housing paintings and sculptures from the end of the 19th century to the present day. (Closed Monday and Tuesday).

MUSEUM OF TURKISH CARPETS
Near the Blue Mosque, it contains a fine collection of Turkish carpets and *kilims*, including some of the oldest examples in existence. (Closed Sunday and Monday).

Mosques

♦♦♦
BLUE MOSQUE (SULTAN AHMET CAMII) ✓

Facing St Sophia is the elegant mosque of Sultan Ahmet I, known as the Blue Mosque because of its magnificent interior of turquoise-blue Iznik tiles. It is the only mosque to have six minarets. Evening *son et lumière* shows in tourist season.

♦♦
SÜLEYMANIYE CAMII

The mosque of Süleyman the Magnificent is considered the most beautiful and splendid of all the imperial mosques in Istanbul. Built between 1550 and 1557, the architect Sinan's goal was to surpass the builders of St Sophia. Standing on a hill, it is conspicuous by its great size, emphasised by the four minarets rising one from each corner of the courtyard. Inside, the *mihrab* (prayer-niche) and *mimber* (pulpit) are of finely-carved white marble, and there are fine stained-glass windows. Adjoining the mosque were theological schools, a school of medicine, a soup kitchen and hospice for the poor, caravanserai and Turkish baths.

♦
FATIH CAMII

This imperial mosque, constructed between 1463 and 1470, bears the name of the conqueror of Istanbul, Fatih Sultan Mehmet II, and is the site of his mausoleum. Standing on top of one of the hills of Istanbul, it is notable for its vast size and

Light pours through 260 windows in the Blue Mosque, second largest in the Moslem world, to highlight the effect of the beautiful porcelain tiles

the religious foundations surrounding it: theological schools, hospices, a hospital, caravanserai, baths and a library.

♦
RÜSTEM PASA CAMII

Built in 1561, the mosque of Rüstem Pasa, beside the Golden Horn, was constructed by the architect Sinan on the orders of Rüstem Pasa, Grand Vizier and son-in-law of Süleyman the Magnificent.

Monuments

♦♦
SULTANAHMET SQUARE

In front of the Blue Mosque is the site of the ancient Hippodrome, scene of chariot races and the

ISTANBUL AND SURROUNDINGS

centre of Byzantine civic life. Of
the monuments which once
decorated it only three remain:
the Obelisk of Theodosius, the
bronze Serpentine Column and
the Column of Constantine.

◆
AHMET III ÇESMESI (FOUNTAIN)

Standing at the entrance to
Topkapı Palace and built in 1729
as a gift to Ahmet III, this is one of
the most magnificent free-
standing fountains in the world.
Highly ornamented and covered
with a pointed roof with deep
eaves, it is a fine example of
fountain architecture.

◆
RUMELI HISARI

The Rumelian Fortress built by
Sultan Mehmet II in 1452 prior to
the conquest of Istanbul was
completed in only four months. It
is now used for some of the
performances that are a feature
of the annual Istanbul Festival.
(Closed Monday).

◆
GALATA KULESI (TOWER)

This huge tower built by the
Genoese in 1348 is 203ft (62m)
high, and now houses a
restaurant and nightclub offering
wonderful views of the Golden
Horn and the Bosphorus.

◆
BEYAZIT KULESI (TOWER)

Situated in the grounds of
Istanbul University, this 279ft
(85m) high tower was built by
Mahmut II in 1828 as a fire tower.

◆◆
ISTANBUL LAND WALLS

Constructed in the 5th century by
the Emperor Theodosius II, the
walls stretch more than 4 miles
(7km) from the Sea of Marmara to
the Golden Horn. With their many
towers and bastions they were
once the mightiest fortifications in
Christendom.

*The Rumeli Hisarı is 6 miles (10km)
north of the city at the narrowest
point of the Bosphorus*

AQUEDUCT OF VALENS (BOZDOGAN KEMERI)

Built by the Emperor Valens in AD368, the aqueduct supplied the Byzantine and later the Ottoman palaces with water. A considerable length of the double-tier arches remains.

◆

KIZ KULESI

Also known as Leander's Tower, this is on a tiny islet at the entrance to Istanbul harbour, though it was across the Hellespont (not the Bosphorus), that Leander swam to Hero – and drowned! Although first constructed in the 12th century, the present building dates from the 18th century.

Hotels

Istanbul has an excellent range of hotels in most price brackets, many located in the Taksim area, the busy centre of the new city. The **Marmara Istanbul** stands on Taksim Square, across from the Atatürk Cultural Centre. A luxury hotel with 432 rooms, its rooftop Panorama Restaurant and Tepe Bar offer splendid panoramas of the city. Across the Taksim Gardens is the **Istanbul Sheraton Hotel & Towers**, which combines the luxury of an international hotel with an Oriental atmosphere. The 429 rooms are handsomely furnished, and the hotel offers a choice of restaurants, La Coupole serving both traditional and local food, and the Revan original Turkish food. Grandly decorated in Ottoman pink, the Revan commands magnificent views of the Bosphorus. Latest addition is the Café Vienna, popular for

coffee, cakes, and ice cream. Close to the Sheraton, on Cumhuriyet Caddesi, is the 200-room **Divan**, whose friendly atmosphere makes it a favourite haunt of Istanbulis. The hotel is famous for its food, be it the delicious chocolates and pastries in the tea-room, the informal fare of the popular Divan Pub, or the international and Turkish cuisine of the stylish Divan Restaurant. From the Divan, a walk along Cumhuriyet Caddesi – the long avenue lined with shops, bars, restaurants, travel agencies and airline offices – leads to the **Istanbul Hilton**, whose spacious gardens and grounds, totalling 13 acres (5.3 hectares), can easily accommodate the hotel's 526 rooms, plus a large convention centre. The Roof Rotisserie commands a panoramic view of the Bosphorus. Also popular are the Hilton's Green House Restaurant and Lalezar Bar. The hotel's sports facilities are excellent and play an important part in the social life of the city. The smaller, 185-room **Maçka** is situated in the fashionable residential district of Macka. It has a good restaurant, and is within easy walking distance of the better shops and restaurants in the area.

Dominating the beautiful bay of Tarabya on the Bosphorus is the luxury **Büyük Tarabya**, a 20-minute drive from the city centre. Its 261 rooms face the bay. The Bogazici Restaurant and the Teras Restaurant are always crowded in the summer.

An airport hotel with a difference is the **Çinar** in Yesilköy. Just 2½ miles (4km) from the airport and 10 miles (16km) from the city, the Çinar has a huge swimming pool and private beach. Its two restaurants are the Mehtap Grill, for Turkish specialities, or the Perigourdine, for dinner and dancing as well as a live show.

For those who prefer the quiet elegance of an Ottoman villa in the heart of the historic city, the **Yesilev**, a beautifully-restored 19th-century mansion, is the place to stay. The 20 high-ceilinged rooms are comfortable and furnished with antiques. A sense of history pervades this small hotel, which is within walking distance of the Topkapı Palace, the Blue Mosque and St Sophia. Two other very stylish hotels converted from interesting old buildings are the **Ayasofia Ottoman Mansions** and the **Sokhollupasa**. The former is, in fact, nine hotels in one: an entire street of old wooden Ottoman houses rescued from destruction and beautifully restored to their past glory. Close to Topkapı Palace and facing St Sophia, the delightful guestrooms, each with its own individual character, are furnished in the gracious style and comfort enjoyed in Ottoman times by rich Turkish families, but now have modern bathrooms. In front of the row of pastel-painted houses runs a steep cobbled street, banned to traffic. The Sokhollupasa, also situated near Topkapı Palace, was built as a mansion for the eminent Sokhollu Pasa, the Ottoman Grand Vizier. Its elegant 18th-century lines have remained unchanged, and inside you will find carved Oriental furniture resting on rich Turkish carpets, a genuine Byzantine wine cellar below

ground, and an original Turkish bath available for the use of hotel guests.

Outside, a gilded staircase sweeps down to the delightful gardens, with a marble fountain. Yet another interesting old building converted into an hotel is **Hidiv Kasri**, once the summer palace of the Egyptian Khedive. Overlooking the Bosphorus, this art deco palace, set in a large park, is for those seeking the opulent Istanbul of the past. The old stables have been converted into a restaurant.

One of Istanbul's oldest hotels, the **Pera Palas**, in the Tepebasi district, overlooking the Golden Horn, was built in 1892 to accommodate passengers on the Orient Express. It is still evocative of a colourful past, while the recently-opened 275-room **Ramada**, in the old city district offers all the modern comforts and facilities associated with international chain hotels. Among the city's other new five-star hotels, the **Çiragan Palas Kempinski**, operated by the German Kempinski group, is outstanding if expensive, and also good is the **Mövenpick**.

Restaurants

Most of the many restaurants to be found in and around the old city are traditional and typically Turkish, such as the **Konyali Palace Restaurant** in Topkapı Palace, whose menu offers excellent, basic Turkish dishes, and delicious savoury pastries and desserts.

The **Gar (station) Restaurant** at Sirkeci Train Station has remained unchanged since 1876, when it proudly greeted

Istanbul is a fine place for shopping, be it street trader, bazaar or high-class international shop

passengers off the legendary Orient Express. Under an impressive, lofty ceiling, both Turkish and international cuisine of a high standard is served. The same management operates the **Borsa Lokantasi**, in the old city, which offers a typical Turkish lunch. For over 60 years it has served simple, freshly prepared Turkish specialities to the business community, and is traditional to the point of not serving alcohol; or, at least, it did not on my last visit.

The huge dining room at the **Liman (port) Lokantasi**, built in 1940, seems so close to the cruise ships lined up on the quay that you have the impression of being able to reach out and touch them. Until the 1950s the Liman catered for the grand receptions

held at the Beylerbeyi and Dolmabahce Palaces and still has a faithful lunchtime clientele. **Beyti**, at Florya, towards the airport, stands beside the Sea of Marmara. Despite its size – 11 dining halls with ceramic tiled walls, 3 terraces and 5 kitchens – this is a culinary institution in Istanbul and one of the best places for Turkish meat dishes. For a typically Oriental flavour, **Pandeli's**, situated above the entrance to the Spice Bazaar, has small, arched rooms decorated with blue tiles. For a magnificent view of the old city, the **Galata Tower's** restaurant at the top of the Genoese (14th-century) Galata Tower is the place to choose. There is also a Turkish nightclub up there.

The atmosphere in the restaurants located in the modern city is more cosmopolitan and less traditional, and the clientele tends to belong to Istanbul's fashionable, international set. **The Plaza** complex, for instance, at Bronz Sokak, close to the Maçka Hotel, is the place where people gather to be seen and to see, and includes an English-style classical bar for cocktails or after-dinner drinks, a light and airy restaurant, and, next door, a discothèque. **Çubuklu 29**, with its stylish art deco interior, comes under the same ownership and has a small restaurant downstairs, specialising in French cuisine; dancing is upstairs. In the summer,Çubuklu 29 moves to Vanikoy 29, on the Asiatic shores of the Bosphorus. A motor-boat is provided for the crossing. **Park Samdan**, in Mim Kemal Oke Caddesi, close to the park, is a smart, modern restaurant decorated with mirrors, and serves excellent Turkish specialities as well as international cuisine. Its sister restaurant, **Samdan 2**, in Nisbetiye Caddesi, is decorated in an art deco style, specialises in Italian food and has a discothèque upstairs.

The **Abdullah Restaurant**, on the hills of Istinye, has been operating since 1881. In the summer, the Abdullah's beautiful garden is a popular spot for eating out, often used by members of the diplomatic corps.

To dine in this watery city is a delight, and the Bosphorus is lined with fish restaurants. Although most of them are good, the **Yeni-Bebek Restaurant**, with its lovely terrace on the Bay of Bebek, is favoured by locals and visitors alike for its seafood specialities. Prices here tend to be high, and in summer it is necessary to book.

The **Ziya** restaurant and bar in Nisantasi is well known for its mezes and is popular with locals, while **Ziya** in Ortaköy attracts a young clientele for dining and dancing by the Bosphorus. Both these are no more than a 20-minute taxi-ride from the city centre.

For the best Turkish show, with Turkish music and exotic belly dancing performances, the place to dine is the **Kervansaray Nightclub**, between the Divan and the Hilton hotels. Others offering Oriental shows are the **Taxim** nightclubs (in Taksim Square and Bebek), where large orchestras accompany the Turkish singers and belly dancers.

Shopping

Istanbul is a good place for shopping, ranging from the bazaars and street markets to fashionable boutiques and shops selling designer clothes.

> **Kapalı Carsı (Covered Bazaar)** ✓

In the old city, the Covered Bazaar, is the largest Oriental souk in the world: a labyrinth of streets and alleys, each specialising in different crafts and trades. The jewellery sections gleam with Oriental pieces in gold or silver, studded with diamonds, gems and precious stones; the copper and bronze section has an amazing array of objects and souvenirs; and the carpet sellers' street provides a luxurious display of colourful wool rugs, fine Hereke silk carpets, old and new woven *kilims*, *cicims* and long-haired goat rugs. In the leather section there is a wide choice of goods, although the quality varies. In the centre of the bazaar is the antique section of the Bedesten, a treasure trove of objects, from ikons, old coins, embroideries, rings, porcelain and onyx vases to weapons, stoves and braziers. Also in the bazaar, antique shops, such as **Abdullah-L.**, **Chalabi** and **Epoque**, have fine ikons, antique jewellery and *objets d'art*. **Berfu** specialises in beautiful handmade jewellery copied from ancient designs up to 5,000 years old. Other shops stocking a large selection of fine jewellery include **Sait Koc**, **Camic** and **Lapis**.

Spice Bazaar

The Spice Bazaar, known as Mısır

The largest covered market in the world, the Covered Bazaar is full of people whose main object in life is to sell something to a tourist

Çarsısı, fills the air with the aroma of herbs and spices, remedial plants, roots and powders; also the place to buy honey, halva, nuts and saffron.

Virtually everywhere you go in Turkey, someone will try to sell you a carpet, and this is especially true in Istanbul. If you are looking for a reliable carpet and rug shop where you can spend some time studying what is available and choosing carefully, with less of the aggressive sales techniques employed by some, go to **Gallery Istanbul**, **Lapis** or **Bazaar 54**.

For a quiet browse and the inevitable glass of tea, go to the shop called **Sofa**, which sells excellent old prints and maps,

calligraphy, old and new Kütahya ceramics, second-hand rugs, *kilims* and Persian miniatures. Shops catering for more contemporary taste and stocking fashionable designer clothes can be found in Istiklal Caddesi, Cumhuriyet Caddesi and the hilly, residential area of Maçka. Some of the city's most elegant shops are in the new galleria complex at Ataköy.

Tourism Bureaux:

Central office: Beyoglu Mesrutiyet Caddesi 57/6, Galatasaray (tel: (1) 2456875, 2433472, 2433731, 2432928). Harbiye: Hilton Hotel (tel: (1) 2330592). Karaköy: Karaköy Limanı Yolcu Salonu (Karaköy Maritime Station) (tel: (1) 2495776). Sultanahmet: Divanyolu Caddesi 3 (tel: (1) 5181802). Yesilköy: Atatürk Hava Limanı (Airport) (tel: (1) 5737399, 5734136).

Excursions from Istanbul

Istanbul is a good base for exploring numerous easily-accessible interesting cities, towns, holiday resorts and islands on the Bosphorus, in the region known as Thrace, and along the Sea of Marmara. If time is at a premium, a day's visit to the Princes' Islands makes a delightful outing. Also popular with visitors are excursions to the holiday resort and thermal spa of Yalova, the town of Iznik, famous for its ceramic tiles, the city of Bursa, and the frontier town of Edirne, provincial capital of European Turkey.

◆◆◆
PRINCES' ISLANDS (KIZIL ADALAR)

A ferry boat trip to one of the Princes' Islands, in the Sea of Marmara, is a pleasant option. Of the 9 islands in total, only 4 are inhabited. Most popular with visitors are Büyükada, which means Big Island, and Heybeliada. Once the pleasure spots of Byzantine princes, they are now popular summer retreats of the city dwellers of Istanbul. On both Büyükada and Heybeliada, restaurants and cafés line the waterfront while, because motor cars are banned, sightseeing is by means of horse-drawn buggies.
Büyükada is arguably the more attractive of these two islands, with the feel of a Mediterranean resort, but both have considerable charm. Popular excursions here from Istanbul involve a morning ferry crossing (from Eminönü), an island buggy tour, followed by lunch in one of the many fish-speciality

restaurants, and finally time for shopping or browsing before taking a late afternoon ferry back to Istanbul. A faster 'sea bus' operates from Kabatas in summer.

◆◆◆
YALOVA

Situated on the southern shore of Marmara, this resort has been attracting visitors since Roman times, thanks to the presence of hot-spring mineral waters flowing from a forested hillside 7 miles (12km) away. The main baths are in Byzantine style, while a large open-air pool is fed by waters that originate at 140°F (60°C). Yalova offers a sandy beach flanked by a pleasant tree-lined promenade, and several modern hotels, while the surrounding hills are particularly popular with walkers and hikers. A summer house built for Atatürk in 1929 is open to visitors. Yalova can be reached from Istanbul by ferry from Sirkeci or the faster 'sea bus' from Kabatas.
Tourism Bureau: Iskele Meydanı 5 (tel: (1931) 2108).

◆◆◆
IZNIK

The town of Iznik is rich in historic monuments. The walls surrounding it, the castle towers and the remains of Roman gates, are all evidence of the city's past importance. The first domed mosque of Ottoman architecture, the Haci Ozbek Camii, the famous tiled Green Mosque, and the Nilüfer Hatun Imareti are among the impressive Islamic monuments to be seen.
First settled in prehistoric times and developed in 316BC by one

of Alexander the Great's generals, Iznik became famous in church history as the meeting place of the First Ecumenical Council which laid down in AD325 the first universally agreed doctrines of Christianity. During the 14th century a porcelain industry was established and this grew rapidly, thanks to constant demand for ceramics to decorate mosques, palaces and other buildings. Among the attractions awaiting visitors to this pleasant town is a 14th-century soup kitchen and a Dervish hospice, now used as a museum featuring, not surprisingly, ceramics.
Tourism Bureau: Kılıçaslan Caddesi 73 (tel: (252) 71933).

◆◆◆
EDIRNE
Edirne, founded by the Roman emperor Hadrian in AD125, is situated on a slope, surrounded by the River Tunca. It is a town of attractive cobbled streets lined with ancient wooden houses, a bustling bazaar, Museum of Turkish and Islamic Art, Archaeological and Ethnographic Museum with many fine Roman statues, and a beautifully-restored caravanserai. One of Edirne's most impressive buildings is Sinan's masterpiece, the Selimiye Mosque, its vast dome surrounded by four immensely tall minarets.
Edirne is also famous for the annual tournament of greased wrestling held in late June and early July on the island of Sarayiçi in the River Tunca, once a hunting reserve for the sultans.
Tourism Bureau: Hürriyet Meydanı 17 (tel: (181) 11518).

◆◆◆
BURSA
There is plenty to see, too, in Bursa, capital of the Ottoman Empire in the 14th century. Among its many impressive Among its many impressive monuments is Yesil Camii, the Green Mosque, built in 1413–21, and considered to be one of the most beautiful in Turkey. Bursa is also renowned as one of Turkey's major health and spa resorts. Standing at the foot of Uludag Mountain, the town is a meeting place for natural, cultural and historic riches. It takes its name from Prusias I, King of Bythinia, and is embellished with many very early examples of Ottoman architecture.
A visit to this green and pleasant town – Turkey's 6th largest with a population of over a million –

The tile decorations in Bursa's Green Mosque are probably the most attractive of any in Turkey

A huge reproduction wooden horse, built according to Homer's description, stands at the entrance to Troy

TROY

Troy (Truva) is evocative of the epic struggle highlighted in *The Iliad*, and was believed to be only a work of Homer's imagination until nine levels of civilisations were unearthed in the 1870s. Heinrich Schliemann found a great deal of treasure at the second from bottom layer (c. 2600BC), which he believed to be Homer's Troy. More recent experts believe that Troy 6 (1900–1300BC) or Troy 7, which was destroyed by an unknown attacker in 1200BC – consistent with the legend of the Trojan War – was the Troy of *The Iliad*. There is not much to see on the site now; there is an interesting museum.
End of excursions

HOW TO GET TO ISTANBUL

By Air

Istanbul's Atatürk Airport is well served by international airlines from most of the world's major capitals. There are connections to the city's domestic airport.

By Road

Coming from Europe, the E5-N (north) enters Turkey from Bulgaria at Kapikule, near Edirne, while the E5-S (south) enters from Greece at Ispala. You enter the old town either through the Topkapı Gate, crossing the Golden Horn by the Atatürk Bridge; or by the Edirnekapi and follow the Fevzipasa Caddesi to the intersection with Atatürk Bulvarı. Visitors staying in hotels in the Taksim Square district or on the Bosphorus may prefer to take the Istanbul bypass at Atatürk Airport, which leads across the Golden Horn Bridge.

should take in the Archaeological Museum, displaying remains from Roman and Byzantine architecture and an interesting coin collection, and the impressive blue-tiled Muradiye Camii, located next to a pretty garden which in summer is ablaze with roses and blossom. Ideally, a visit to Bursa would not be complete without an ascent of Uludag, especially in springtime when the hillsides are ablaze with blossoms and wild flowers. A cable car operates from the hillside to the east of the town, or you can take a taxi up the mountain road from Çekirge. The view from the top is magnificent.
Tourism Bureau: Belediye Alt Geçit Çarşısı 1, Orhan Gazi Parkı (tel: (24) 212359). Near the Ulu Mosque.

THE BLACK SEA

Turkey's Black Sea shores are not as developed touristically as her Aegean and Mediterranean coasts, but with their densely forested mountains giving way to tea terraces, hazel-nut groves and tobacco plantations, and pleasant seaside resorts, they are becoming increasingly popular with international visitors. According to legend, these shores, cut off from the rest of Turkey by the Black Sea mountain chain, were the land of the mighty Amazons, and an Amazon queen is said to have founded Sinop, famous as the birthplace of the satirist and philosopher Diogenes.

The most developed of the many coastal resorts along the Black Sea include Kilyos and Sile, not far from Istanbul, while other towns with good beaches include Akcakoca, Inkum, Amasra and Fatsa. The region is also home to the busy port of Trabzon, set in spectacular scenery, and with a rich historical heritage. Here, there are the remains of a Byzantine fortress and many ancient buildings, including the church of St Sophia (now a museum) with its interesting frescoes and reliefs. Not far from Trabzon is the Monastery of Sumela, set like a swallow's nest on a sheer rock face.

The southern coast of the Black Sea was for centuries one of the world's busiest maritime highways. As early as 1250BC it was the route taken by the Argonauts sailing out of the Bosphorus eastwards over the perennially dark waters of this inland sea, on their way to Colchis in search of the Golden Fleece. The coast was an avenue of escape for Xenophon the Athenian and what was left of his Ten Thousand, fighting their way back home to Greece in 401–399BC. In 1295 Marco Polo,

Blue water and blue sky on the Black Sea at Sile

THE BLACK SEA

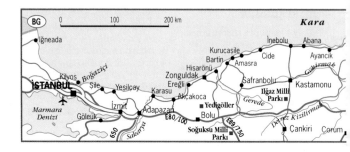

with his career in Cathay behind him, took ship at Trapezus, later Trebizond and now Trabzon, and sailed to Constantinople (now Istanbul) and at last to Italy. Kingdoms flourished and died here, like that of Mithridates the Great who defied and then succumbed to the power of Imperial Rome, and Byzantine Trabzon itself which survived Constantinople by almost a decade.

The Black Sea coast's isolation has made it strikingly different from the rest of Turkey, physically and culturally. It is cut off from the hot summers and severe winters of Anatolia by the mountains that rise parallel to the coast to heights of between 1,968 and 9,842ft (600 and 3,000m) and give the coastal zone the highest rainfall of any part of Turkey, reflected by the fertility of the land.

◆
KILYOS
A snug little seaside village located some 22 miles (35km) from Istanbul and about 6 miles (10km) from the Bosphorus, Kilyos has a lovely, long wide beach of golden sand, and several hotels, restaurants, bars

and shops. In the close vicinity is some lovely scenery with many small farms scattered across the lush green fields, making this ideal walking country.

Hotels
One of the nicest hotels in the resort is the **Gurup**, small and inexpensive.

◆
SAMSUN
Samsun, called Amisos by its founders, shows no evidence of its violent past: in the first century BC its citizens burned Amisos down rather than surrender to the Romans who had laid siege to them. Fourteen centuries later the city was once again burned to the ground, this time by the Genoese traders of Amisos defending themselves from the Ottomans. Modern Turkey was born at Samsun on 19 May 1919 when a young officer from Macedonia called Mustafa Kemal, later known as Atatürk, stepped ashore here from the steamer *Bandirma* to lead his struggling armies across Anatolia to victory at Smyrna (Izmir). He went on to form the first Turkish republic and bring the country into the 20th century, something that

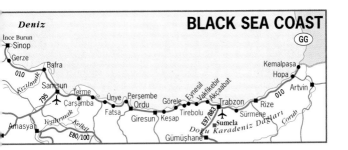

BLACK SEA COAST

Deniz

Samsun certainly reflects today with its sprawling annual trade and industrial fair.
Tourism Bureau: 19 Mayıs Mah, Talimhane Caddesi 6 (tel: (36) 152887).

◆◆
SILE
Sile has long been a popular resort with Turkish people, and is now also attracting foreign visitors with its lovely beach and easy-going atmosphere. A hotch-potch of windows and balconies look down on the harbour, beaches, pedal-boats, board-sailers and bathers. There are many pleasant restaurants facing the main street, most of them offering tables with sea-views. The sea is warm and clear, and the sand perfect. The main beaches are also well equipped and, small bars provide hot snacks, cold drinks and music.
A hike to the caves, coves, bays and beaches adjacent to Sile will stretch the fittest muscles, or alternatively you can take an inexpensive *dolmus* taxi. Outside the resort are secluded places, most with simple refreshment facilities. Least energetic of excursions on foot is one to the

local lighthouse, Turkey's biggest, dating back to 1858. It is worth the walk for the views from its base and depending which of the keepers is on duty, you may be able to enjoy a tour of the house and a bird's-eye view of Sile. For the evenings, beach barbecues where you make your own entertainment are more popular than discothèques, although there are a couple of simple nightspots in the resort.

Hotels
The inexpensive **Degirmen** by the beach, offers 73 rooms with private facilities and balconies, a restaurant and bars.

◆◆◆
TRABZON
Trabzon remains the metropolis of the eastern Black Sea coast, and it was here that the last Byzantine emperor watched land and sea for the coming of the Ottoman Turks. The 350-year-old empire of Trebizond, as it was once known, perished on 15 August 1561 after the Turkish Sultan Mehmet II subjected the city to the same total defeat he had inflicted on Constantinople only eight years before.

THE BLACK SEA

In 13th-century St Sophia, there are many beautiful paintings and gold mosaics on walls and ceiling

Enough still remains of the legendary 'towers of Trebizond' to conjure up what the Imperial city must have been like. The city's churches, once the pride and glory of ancient Christendom, were converted to Moslem worship and as a result have survived in better condition. At the Church of the Golden Headed Virgin, now the Ortahisar or Fatih Mosque, the cupola is still plated with gold. The church of St Sophia, the 'Holy Wisdom' of Trebizond, now a museum, is the best-preserved example of Byzantine architecture on this coast.

In the wild mountains steeply rising south of Trabzon, an astonishingly varied fauna persists in the native forest of beech, alder, oak and wild nut trees. Chamois, brown bear, jackal, wild cat, ibex, mountain goat, otter, marten and wild boar are all to be found here (see also page 101).

Tourism Bureau: Vilayet Binasi, Kat 4 (tel: (031) 235833/235818).

HOW TO GET TO THE BLACK SEA COAST

Flights operate from Istanbul and Ankara to Samsun and Trabzon. By train, the Eastern Express goes from Istanbul via Erzurum to Kars, from where you can continue by bus. There are also bus connections to all provincial centres, while Turkish Maritime Lines operates services from Istanbul to Zonguldak, Sinop, Samsun, Giresun, Trabzon and Rize (departing Mondays from early June to late September), a journey that takes two days.

EASTERN TURKEY

The eastern region of Turkey, with the Taurus Mountains in the south and the chain of the Black Sea mountains in the north encircling the Anatolian Plateau to form a mighty, complex mountain range, is a diverse land which differs significantly from the rest of the country.

Visitors here will be amazed by the variety of the landscape: the red ochre plateau of Erzurum; the forests, waterfalls and green pastures of Kars and Agri; the never-melting snow of Mount Agri; the immense Lake Van with its deep blue waters; the torrid plain of High Mesopotamia; and the fertile valleys of the Dicle (Tigris) and Fırat (Euphrates). Historic treasures of the region are likewise full of variety; the astounding sanctuary of Antiochus I, with its colossal statues, at Nemrut Dağı (Mountain); Byzantine monasteries and churches; mausoleums and caravanserais of the Seljuk period; elegant Ottoman mosques; and hilltop fortresses. As the battlefront of Eastern and Western cultures represented by the Romans and Parthians and the Byzantines and Sassanids, culminating in the final conquest of Anatolia by an Eastern people, the Seljuk Turks, the region has had an active past. In the area where the central steppe gives way to the more mountainous terrain of the east are the important Seljuk centres of Sivas, Divrigi, Eski Malatya and Harput, all of which possess monuments testifying to the brilliant achievements of Seljuk art. Situated at a height of 6,398ft

(1,950m) is Erzurum, in which are mosques and mausoleums of the Seljuk and Mongol periods, and the well-preserved walls of a Byzantine fortress. To the north is the much fought-over frontier city of Kars, dominated by a formidable fortress, and nearby are the ruins of 10th-century Ani. Mount Ararat, (Agri Dağı) Turkey's highest mountain, is where Noah's Ark is believed to have come to rest. It is also where history is thought to have begun, and stands as a dividing point between nations and empires. At the base of this mountain is the intriguing 17th-century mosque and palace of Ishak Pasa at Doğubayazıt. On the banks of the immense and beautiful Lake Van is the city of

Nemrut Dağı is the 2,000-year-old site of a tomb sanctuary, consisting of a series of enormous stone statues

EASTERN TURKEY

the same name, with its Urartu citadel dating back to the first millennium BC and mosques and mausoleums of the Seljuk and Ottoman periods.

In the region that was once Upper Mesopotamia in the basin of the Dicle (Tigris) and Firat (Euphrates) are the cities of Diyarbakır, Mardin and Sanliurfa, all former centres of the Hurri-Mitani in the second millennium BC.

Finally, north of Adıyaman in the mountain vastness of the southeast is one of Turkey's most spectacular monuments, the funerary sanctuary of Nemrut Dagı, with its colossal toppled heads of gods, which was erected 2,000 years ago for King Antiochus I.

Life in the region is generally austere, and hotels display little concession towards sophistication, so visitors here must be prepared for simple if not basic standards, and a certain degree of 'roughing' it. It is wise, also, to choose the time of your visit carefully because, due to the altitude and lack of sea influence, the climate of eastern Turkey is one of extremes: dry, hot summers and harsh, severe winters. The climate is even more extreme in the northeast, where winters are long and bitter and the summers merely warm; the southeast boasts scorching summers and short, mild winters.

◆◆◆
DIYARBAKIR

Diyarbakır is one of the most attractive cities in eastern Turkey. Situated on a plateau, it is characterised by triple black basalt walls that encircle the old town, giving it a medieval aspect. These ramparts, which have 16 keeps and 5 gates, are among the longest in the world. They were built by the Emperor Constantius, son of Constantine the Great, in AD349, have been kept in a constant state of good repair and are still in excellent condition along their entire length.

Also of interest in the city is the Ulu Mosque, notable for its original architecture and the amount of ancient materials used in the restoration of the building at various times. There is also an interesting archaeological museum housed in a former

theological college, with exhibits covering some 4,000 years.

Hotels
Recommended hotels include the **Demir** and the **Diyarbakır Büyük**.
Tourism Bureau: Lise Caddesi, Onur Apt Altı 24/A (tel: (831) 12173).

◆◆◆
MARDIN
Whereas Diyarbakır is a city of

The famous 10th-century Church of the Holy Cross on Akdamar Island, 25 miles (41km) from Van, is the world's finest example of medieval Armenian architecture

black appearance due to the basalt used in the old walls, Mardin, which overlooks the vast Mesopotamian plain, is a city of white aspect because of its limestone buildings. Of particular interest in the city is its Roman citadel. This was reputedly impregnable, a claim supported by the fact that neither the Seljuks in the 12th century nor the Mongols in the 13th century managed to capture it. The only one who did was Tamerlane, in the 14th century.

Various Islamic monuments include the 15th-century Kasım Pasa Medrese; the Latifiye Mosque and the Ulu Mosque, built in the 11th century by the Seljuks; and the Sultan Isa Medrese, which has a finely-decorated portal.

Four miles (7km) from Mardin, on the road to Akinci, lies the great Syriac-Jacobite monastery of Deyrulzaferan, while at nearby Kızıltepe is one of the best examples of Artukid architecture, the 13th-century Ulu Mosque.
Tourism Bureau: Meydanbası Caddesi, Il Halk Kütüphanesi (tel: (841) 11665).

◆◆
LAKE VAN
Lake Van is by far the largest lake in Turkey – five times the size of Lake Geneva, for instance – and is astonishingly beautiful: an inland sea at an altitude of nearly 6,000ft (1,830m) ringed by the towering mountains of eastern Anatolia. The lake contains sulphur springs at a depth of 300ft (91m) along the shore and 600ft (183m) in the centre, which give an excessively high salt content to the water, not unlike

the Dead Sea. In winter, fierce and unpredictable storms make navigation impossible. In summer, however, the lake is becoming increasingly popular.

The modern town of Van, which lies about 3 miles (5km) distant inland from the lakeshore, is a delightful place not yet taken over by tourists, although it seems only a matter of time before it will be. For the present, its pleasant restaurants and *lokantas* are refreshingly free from the usual tourist influences. The uninhabited old city is situated at the foot of a massive rock platform. Here the citadel, 1¾ miles (3km) west of the new town, dominates the ruins of old churches, of Seljuk and Ottoman mosques, and the homes that are hollowed out of sheer rock. An excellent museum in Van contains fine examples of Urartian arts and crafts.

At Çavustepe, 15 miles (25km) from Van, there is an important Urartian site with temples, a palace and inscriptions; and in Hosap, 37 miles (60km) distant, there is an interesting 17th-century castle.

Tourism Bureau: Cumhuriyet Caddesi 19, Van (tel: (061) 63675).

♦♦♦
NEMRUT DAGI ✓

Nemrut Dagı (mountain) is the site of the extraordinary tomb-sanctuary erected 2,000 years ago by King Antiochus I of the Commagenes, the most renowned monarch of a land which encompassed what today is the region of Adıyaman, Maras and Gaziantep.

The monarchs of Commagenes were regarded as gods, and considered themselves as such – and none more so than Antiochus I, who had a group of enormous stone statues erected at the summit of the mountain 'in commemoration of my own glory and of that of the gods'. An act of megalomania, it must have involved an army of slaves toiling for many years to hump the huge stones to the mountain's summit. Over the years the colossal statues, 25–35ft (7.6–10.7m) in height, have suffered from the ravages of time, earthquakes and erosion, but the site is still extremely impressive, especially if viewed at either dawn or dusk. Nemrut Dagı is reached from either the town of Adıyaman, 53 miles (86km) away, where a jeep and driver can be hired, or the nearer village of Kahta, where accommodation is also available. For those who make the ascent in late afternoon, primitive lodgings are available on the peak itself.

Tourism Bureau: Atatürk Bulvarı 184, Adıyaman (tel: (878) 13151).

HOW TO GET TO EASTERN TURKEY

Turkish Airlines operates frequent services from Istanbul and Ankara to various centres in Eastern Turkey, including Diyarbakır and Van.

By train, the Eastern Express runs between Istanbul –Erzincan–Erzurum–Kars, while the Vangölü train runs between Istanbul Malatya–Elazig– Mus–Tatvan and on by ferry to Van. There are also inexpensive bus services from Istanbul and Ankara to all principal towns in the region.

PEACE AND QUIET:

Wildlife and Countryside in Turkey
by Paul Sterry

Turkey is steeped in history and rich in wildlife. It has played host to many cultures and civilisations over the last three centuries, and yet much of it is still relatively wild and unspoilt.

Although only 3 per cent of the country lies in Europe, it still boasts most of the species of plant, bird and mammal that are found in adjacent countries like Greece. However, on the Asian side of the Bosphorus, many birds reach their western-most limit, seldom crossing the narrow, watery divide. This strategic position has made the isthmus separating Asia and Europe of immense importance to migrating birds, which pass through Turkey each year in their millions.

The countryside is extraordinarily varied. In spring, the extensive coastlines of the Black and Aegean Seas are a riot of colour; much of the inland area is dominated by the Anatolian plateau, parts of which are high enough to reach the snow line; the extensive wooded slopes are still the haunt of bears and wolves.

Aleppo pines are the most common pines along the Turkish coast. Their shape is usually distinctive

PEACE AND QUIET

Coasts and Sea

The extensive coastline is largely
unspoilt, and until comparatively
recently was unknown to the
majority of tourists. Much of the
coast is rugged and mountainous
and is cloaked in woodland
which drops down to sandy
beaches between rocky
headlands. Fortunately, some of
the best areas have been
protected from future
development by being given
national park status. The Dilek
peninsula on the Aegean Sea,
which is close to Ephesus and
Izmir, is particularly outstanding.
Its jagged hills rise from sea level
to a height of over 3,937ft
(1,200m), providing a wonderful
setting for its many
archaeological treasures and
wildlife. Birds of prey haunt the
slopes, and rare and secretive
mammals like jackal, striped
hyena, wild boar and porcupine
are found here. Even leopards
are not unknown in Dilek, but to
see one of these beautiful animals
you will need to be well off the
beaten track and extremely
lucky.

The national park at Olympos-
Bey Dağları protects a stretch of
coast running west from the Gulf
of Antalya which is also
impressively scenic. Mountains
rising to over 6,562ft (2,000m)
and covered in Calabrian pines
provide a stunning backdrop for
wonderful sandy beaches. From
here you may see parties of
shearwaters flying by in long
formations. Corys are common,
and are often joined by the
smaller eastern Mediterranean
race of the Manx shearwater,
known as the Levantine
shearwater.

*Slender-billed gulls can sometimes
be seen around the Turkish coasts*

At certain times of the year, gulls
can be common around the
shores. Little and Mediterranean
gulls both sport neat, black hoods
and white wings during the
breeding season. They are easy
to tell apart, however, because
the little gull is considerably
smaller and has underwings
which are almost black. Smaller
numbers of slender-billed gulls
also pass through the region.
They have white heads
throughout the year and a close
view will reveal their unusual
pale eyes.

Try visiting the coastal area
around Miletus to the south of
Izmir; it lies at the mouth of the
Menderes River. Inland is Lake
Bafa which is good for wetland
wildlife. Termessos (Güllük Dağı)
National Park, on the Gulf of
Antalya, includes Mount Güllük
and has Mediterranean flowers
as well as bears and jackals. The
nearby port of Tasucu is good for
gulls and waders.

In and Around Istanbul

The narrow strip of water known
as the Bosphorus, now neatly

spanned by a bridge, is the dividing line between Asia and Europe. The waters of the Bosphorus run northeast into the Black Sea and southwest through the Sea of Marmara into the Mediterranean; so, not surprisingly, Istanbul has been an important trading post for centuries. The Bosphorus is also an important route for many seabirds, and incredible numbers of Levantine shearwaters pass through each day.

Istanbul's cosmopolitan atmosphere attracts not only people from far away, but birds as well. Alpine swifts, with their neat black and white plumage, scream overhead, while palm doves peck the ground for seeds and crumbs. These neat little pigeons are widespread in Africa, and Istanbul is their most northerly outpost. Black kites,

ubiquitous scavengers of warmer climates, are to be seen everywhere. They will daringly dive down on to the pavement to pick up a scrap of food and often congregate around market places.

Istanbul is also on the migration route for many birds flying from Africa to northern Europe and Asia. Parks and gardens in and around the city provide a welcome stopping-off point for tired migrants and a single tree may hold up to six species on a good day during migration time. For peace and quiet in Istanbul visit the gardens of the Topkapı Palace – called Gülhane Park – which lie on Kennedy Caddesi close to the Bosphorus. Look for migrant birds in spring and autumn here and in Yıldız Park on

Despite their camouflage, Turkish geckos are often caught

PEACE AND QUIET

*Red-footed falcons are among
Turkey's most common birds
of prey*

Ciragan Caddesi.
Travel northwest from the city
and you soon reach open country
often heavily grazed by goats
and sometimes cultivated.
Overlooking the fields and scrub,
the wires and fences which line
the roads provide excellent
perches for red-footed falcons,
lesser kestrels, shrikes and bee-
eaters. Their keen eyes are ever
alert for the slightest movement
below, which would give away
the presence of an insect or a
lizard. Turkish geckos are
frequent victims and are
abundant in the undergrowth,
sometimes even venturing inside
buildings.

Birds over the Bosphorus
Istanbul's unique position has
aided its prosperity throughout
the ages, but it has also made it of
immense strategic importance to
migrating birds. Each spring and
autumn, millions of birds pass
over the skies of Istanbul on their
way to and from their wintering
grounds in Africa.
The reason for the concentration
of large birds of prey and storks
through the region is simple.
Most large birds migrate by day,
using thermals to give them lift
and assist their passage, and so
avoid crossing seas and oceans
wherever possible, because very
little heat rises off the water. The
narrow isthmus on which Istanbul
is sited effectively provides a
land bridge between the
Mediterranean and the Black Sea.
The only thing standing in the
way of the birds' migration route
is the narrow strip of water called
the Bosphorus, and so every
morning in spring and autumn
birds congregate in the skies
over the hills around the
Bosphorus, gathering enough
height to glide over the water.

The thousands of birds which pass through each day provide a memorable spectacle. Although you can witness impressive migration almost anywhere around Istanbul, the Camlica hills on the Asiatic side of the Bosphorus are generally considered to give the best vantage point. From March until May the skies are full of Levant sparrowhawks, honey buzzards, black kites and lesser-spotted eagles. Their numbers are supplemented by red-footed falcons, lesser kestrels, booted eagles and harriers, and both white and black storks are a daily feature, sometimes numbering into the thousands. The same spectacle can be witnessed in the autumn, from August until October, but at this season, of course, the migration is in the other direction. Although autumn migration is perhaps not as concentrated as that in spring, the young birds of that year swell the numbers to unbelievable proportions.
If possible, time your arrival on the Çamlıca hills to just after dawn.
The best site from which to watch migrating birds at the Bosphorus is on the Büyük Camlica hill at Kisikli. The café on the hilltop makes an ideal spot to enjoy this wildlife spectacle while sipping Turkish coffee and eating breakfast.

Hills and Mountains

Much of the central region of Turkey is dominated by the hilly Anatolian plateau which still holds vast tracts of wild and unspoilt country. Much of the land is more than 3,281ft (1,000m) above sea level and in places it rises much higher. Bolkar Dag, east of Antalya, rises to over 10,800ft (3,300m), while Mount Ararat (or Agri) widely held to be the resting place of Noah's Ark, reaches 16,945ft (5,165m) on the Russian border.

Many of the more exciting areas are to all intents and purposes inaccessible. However, areas like Kovada Lake at the western end of the Taurus Mountain range have received national park status to protect them. Although close to the sea, the wooded slopes make a refreshing change from the coast, and the oaks and Calabrian pines provide shelter for red and roe deer, wild boar and wolves. Although nearly hunted to extinction, small numbers of European brown bears survive here and in other remote regions. Sadly, a few are still trained and kept as 'dancing bears', a degrading occupation for one of Europe's most magnificent animals.

The open slopes are the haunts of golden eagles, which glide effortlessly on their immense wings over the broken terrain. Although they will feed on carrion, they are adept at hunting for themselves, and chukars (a species of partridge) are an important part of their diet. Vultures, on the other hand, feed almost exclusively on animal remains and seldom kill anything for themselves. Griffon, black and Egyptian vultures, are all likely to be seen in the wilder regions and are sometimes joined by the majestic lammergeier, with its long tapering wings.

Rocky gullies and gorges are the favoured nesting sites for rock

PEACE AND QUIET

thrushes and blue rock thrushes, the latter with its slaty-blue plumage looking dull in comparison to the gaudy male rock thrush. Despite its vivid colours, the rock thrush is often not spotted until it flies, when its white rump is conspicuous. The Lake Kovada National Park lies in the western Taurus mountains in southern Anatolia and the best time is from May until September. Another good mountain area is around Baldaras, which is on the E98. Alpine flowers and birds abound in the springtime. Look for vultures, eagles, larks and wheatears as well as wallcreepers, which feed on cliff faces and gorges.

European brown bears are still found in small numbers in prime woodland

Woodlands
Woodlands remain widespread in Turkey and provide cool shade for both walker and wildlife. In central areas of Turkey especially, the forests help moderate the extremes in temperature, remaining cool in summer and providing shelter in winter. Coastal areas and the lower slopes of the hills often have deciduous trees such as oak, chestnut, plane and beech, while pines and firs prefer the higher reaches.

Just outside Istanbul, on the European side of the Bosphorus, lies the Belgrade Forest, a largely deciduous area of oak and ash. Bright yellow and orange Cleopatra butterflies flit along the glades, while Hungarian gliders live up to their name and race along. In spring, the trees come alive with a chorus of nightingales, blackcaps and golden orioles, but hearing them will prove much easier than seeing them as they flit through the dappled leaf canopy.

Honey buzzards are secretive nesters in the highest branches of the trees. They are easiest to see early in the season, just after their arrival from Africa, when they soar overhead in display flights showing their characteristic barred underwings. As their name implies, their favourite food is to be found in the underground nests of wild bees and wasps. You may spot the tell-tale excavations along forest rides where the nests have been raided, but it is not the honey that the buzzards consume, but insect larvae. In the skies above the

Dense woodland is home to the Syrian woodpecker

woods, they are often joined by hobbies acrobatically catching insects on the wing. The mountains of the Taurus range on Turkey's southern coast, as well as the Anatolian plateau, still support vast areas of prime woodland, despite forest clearance and damage by grazing animals. Yedigöller, northwest of Ankara, is a national park containing both deciduous and coniferous woodland between 2,297 and 4,921ft (700 and 1,500m) above sea level. Deer and wild boar roam these woods and wolves and brown bears occur in small numbers. The Belgrade Forest can be reached by driving northwest from Istanbul towards Kilyas. Numerous forest paths start from the road and the further you walk away from the road the more wildlife you are likely to find. Never leave valuables in your unattended car.

Agricultural Land

Farmland in Turkey is a botanist's delight. Because the farming is less intensive and herbicides seldom used, the so-called cornfield 'weeds', now a thing of the past in many other countries, abound. Throughout the spring and summer, corn marigolds, mayweeds, cornflowers, poppies, pheasant's eye and borage offer a whole spectrum of colours and are enthusiastically visited by numerous bees and butterflies. If there are orchards nearby, then black-veined whites and scarce swallowtails, and butterflies whose caterpillars feed on the leaves of fruit trees, will be frequent and conspicuous visitors.

Olives are commonly grown in Turkey, and ancient groves of gnarled and twisted trees are a familiar sight. Their leaves provide shade and shelter for olive tree and olivaceous warblers, large birds by the standards of other warblers, with loud, harsh alarm calls and songs.

Olive groves and orchards are often grazed by goats, which soon create a disturbed and dusty soil. Although this may not suit many animals and plants, it is very much to the liking of resident and migrant pipits and larks. The sandy-coloured tawny pipit feeds alongside crested and short-toed larks which search for small insects and seeds among the broken soil. Wherever there are overhead wires in Turkey you will find birds perching on them. Colourful bee-eaters and bright blue rollers use these man-made lookouts to scan the ground below for insects and

PEACE AND QUIET

A typical small Turkish farm, with a patchwork of habitats

other small animals. Bee-eaters prefer to catch bees and dragonflies in flight, while rollers drop to the ground to secure grasshoppers or even small lizards. They are often joined on the wires by black-headed buntings, bright yellow birds with smart, black caps which use the perches to advertise their territories with their songs.

Open Country

Centuries of woodland clearance and grazing by goats have produced tracts of open, barren country. For most of the year the land is a uniform sandy brown, with the dried remains of plants and only the occasional evergreen shrub like kermes oak to break the monotony. However, for a couple of months in spring, the fields come alive with colourful plants such as asphodel, tassel hyacinths and a whole range of orchids, and tree

grayling and Amanda's blue butterflies feast on the nectar. Spring is also the time when reptiles are at their most conspicuous. Wall lizards bask in the early morning sun and spur-thighed tortoises noisily plod through the vegetation.

Dry, barren fields are the favoured haunt of wheatears. These alert little birds all share the same upright stance as they hop along the ground and a conspicuous white rump when they fly. Several species pass through Turkey on migration but two commonly stay to breed in these open habitats. Black-eared wheatears have a pale body with contrasting black wings and cheeks, and some adult males even have a black throat making them look most distinguished. The isabelline wheatear, which is a pale, uniform sandy colour all over and has longer legs than other wheatears, is also common in Asiatic Turkey, although it is almost unknown on the other side of the Bosphorus.

Spur-Thighed Tortoise

Spur-thighed tortoises are a common sight in meadows and open country in the spring. Often the first sign of their presence is a loud rustling in the vegetation. The female lays about 10 or 12 eggs (which have hard shells) in the soil and these incubate in the heat of the sun. When the young tortoises hatch they are just like miniature adults. They may grow rather slowly but after several years the shell may be more than 10in (25 cm) in length. Spur-thighed tortoises feed on plant material, although they will sometimes eat small animals or carrion. They get their name from the presence of small spurs on the back of the thighs.

Regrettably tortoises are still collected for the pet trade, although many countries have banned the import and sale of wild tortoises. In wilder, more remote areas, jackals still roam the open country. Although wisely distrustful of man, they can sometimes be seen trotting in the distance and in the evenings, their long, drawn-out howls a reminder of the untamed nature of much of Turkey. Long-legged buzzards also populate this bleak terrain, rising on thermals above rocky outcrops and cliffs. They share the air with many other similar-sized birds of prey but they are the only species with an unbarred, buff tail.

Lakes and Marshes

Inland of the southern shore of the Sea of Marmara there are large lakes which lie within easy reach of Istanbul. The most westerly of these is Lake Manyas, south of Bandırm. The lake is low-lying, being only 33ft (10m) above sea level, and has extensive reedbeds with willow scrub, which support vast numbers of breeding herons and egrets. Among the trees, mixed colonies of pygmy cormorant, spoonbill and glossy ibis nest in May and June. The ibises are often seen probing the muddy margins in search of food; in flight, they have a conspicuously bulbous head. The northeast shore of Lake Manyas forms Kuscenneti (Bird Paradise) National Park with more than 200 species of bird. There is a museum and organised birdwatching tours. The best time to visit is from March to October. Also visit Lake Ulubat, south of the road (route 2) from Bursa to Bandırma. Waterbirds abound and migrants feed around the margin. Lake Iznik, southwest of Izmir, is also rich in bird life and this spectacle is

Marshes and low-lying land are home to many reptiles, including the painted frog

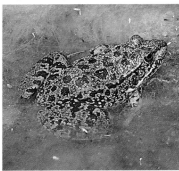

improved by the stunning, mountainous backdrop. In the extensive reedbeds, tree frogs keep up an all-day chorus, seemingly oblivious to the heat of the sun. Deep in the cover of the reeds, purple herons and little bitterns rear their young, but are seldom seen except when in flight. Fish are abundant in the shallow waters and, consequently, most of the larger birds feed almost exclusively on them. In the open water, flocks of white and Dalmatian pelicans glide gracefully sometimes scooping the water with the capacious beaks.

Lying so close to the migration route through the Bosphorus and close to the sea, the lakes of northwest Turkey are important stopping-off points for migrants. In the spring, Caspian and white-winged black terns boost the numbers of breeding whiskered terns, and many migrant storks drop in to feed for a day or two. Further around the coast, rivers that run down to the sea often create marshes and pools. Although smaller in scale than the lakes near Istanbul, they can nevertheless hold considerable wildlife interest. Painted frogs and tree frogs are sometimes found in such places, attracting herons and egrets if the site is undisturbed, and during spring and autumn, migrants can drop in at any time.

Uludag National Park

Lying to the south of the town of Bursa in northern Asiatic Turkey, the Uludag National Park embraces the southern slopes of Mount Uludag. This rises from land below 1,640 ft (500m) to the summit at 8,343ft (2,543m) above sea level, but fortunately a road zig-zags its way up the slope. As an added bonus, the traveller passes through all the major environmental zones found in Turkey, from Mediterranean maquis all the way to the snow line.

On the lower slopes and on the fringes of cultivated areas, rock roses, lavenders and kermes oak, the latter with leaves like miniature holly, brighten the landscape wherever the goats have failed to graze. Colourful members of the bee orchid family, with their furry, chestnut and pink flowers, grow out of even the barest earth, and insects such as the mantis fly throng through the air.

As the road climbs, it passes through varied woodland containing beech, laurel, chestnut, firs and pines. This mixture of tree species attracts a variety of woodland birds, from warblers to black woodpeckers. Birds of prey nest in the high tree canopies and soar overhead during the heat of the day. The woods also provide a safe haven for mammals like brown bear, wild boar, jackal and wolf, who do not often venture out of cover before nightfall.

Uludag is also a ski resort during the winter, and near the summit, hotels, ski lifts and cable railways bear witness to its popularity. Despite this disturbance, however, inaccessible crags and gullies provide feeding areas and nesting sites for rock thrushes and rock sparrows, while shore larks and alpine accentors are often seen.

The skies over the mountain are the realm of vultures and eagles.

The elegant, adult mantis fly is a resident of rocky hillsides and abandoned farmland

Griffon vultures rise on the first thermals of the day and their broad wings can keep them aloft for hours on end. Golden and Bonelli's eagles are also frequently seen, the latter with a remarkably quick turn of speed when needed.

To reach Uludag National Park drive south 22 miles (35km) from Bursa. Within the park there are numerous hotels and campsites. There are trails and footpaths – ask for details in the hotels – as well as ski-lifts and cable cars. Skiing is popular in winter and the park itself is open from June to September.

Turtles

Turkey is one of the last countries bordering the Mediterranean which still supports a mainland breeding population of loggerhead turtles. Disturbance and tourist development have caused them to desert all but the most remote island sites elsewhere in Europe; and with Turkey's ever-growing tourist industry, how long will they remain here?

The loggerhead turtles' dilemma is that they traditionally lay their eggs on the same sandy beaches that have recently become so attractive to people. Although they visit the sites at night, when the beaches are comparatively deserted by tourists, inconsiderate behaviour can cause them to retreat back to the water without laying their eggs, never to return to the beach again. The eggs, which are left to incubate in the sand for nearly two months, are also vulnerable to digging and trampling, and if the turtles are to survive they must be given precedence over people in certain critical sites. The beach at Dalyan, near Fethiye in southwest Turkey, is now the only major nesting beach in the country and it is still visited by nearly 300

PEACE AND QUIET

Turtles are pitifully vulnerable when on land

animals a year. It ranks as the second most important site, after the Greek island of Zakynthos, in the whole of the Mediterranean. Conservation bodies have managed to persuade the Turkish authorities that this site is of such importance that it must be saved, and the beach and its surroundings have recently been declared a national conservation area. Hopefully, the authorities will soon realise that there is also money to be made from the presence of the turtles: with careful guidance and supervision, large numbers of people can watch these magnificent animals laying their eggs, without causing them undue distress.

During the egg-laying season turtles are often seen off shore in the bays and coves which adorn the Turkish coast, and to see them swimming in the sea is to see them in their element. On land their movements are woefully inadequate and they are barely able to haul their great shells up the beaches. At sea, however, they literally 'fly' through the water and are as graceful as any bird in flight, their long, paddle-like flippers powering them along.

The Waldrapp

The small town of Birecik, which lies on the River Firat (Euphrates) close to the Syrian border, is host to the last remaining site, not only in Turkey but also in Eurasia, for the waldrapp or bald ibis. The colony, which now only nests off the rock faces surrounded by the village itself, is in great danger of extinction.

Waldrapps spend the spring in and around Birecik, feeding in the few remaining marshy meadows in the vicinity of the village and nesting on rock ledges. After July, however, they disperse to their wintering grounds in the Middle East and north Africa.

Formerly threatened by hunting and now by the use of pesticides and changes in land use, the population in Birecik had dwindled to 13 birds by 1984. A similar pattern of decline has occurred in the waldrapp's other colonies in Morocco and Algeria, with the entire population being no more than a few hundred strong, and its prospects seem bleak. Perhaps the only long-term future for this bizarre bird, which was once recorded in ancient Egyptian hieroglyphics, is in captivity, where it breeds with some success.

FOOD AND DRINK

It is worth going to Turkey just for the food which is fresh and nutritious, with large, healthy amounts of grains and pulses used in the dishes, often topped with delicious creamy yoghurt. Lamb is the basic meat of Turkish cooking whether in casseroles, as spicy meatballs (*köfte*), as the famous *sis kebap* – charcoal grilled on a skewer – or *döner kebaps* served in pitta bread. Fish, which is priced in restaurants according to individual size, is usually fresh from the day's catch. *Barbunya* (red mullet), *kılıç balığı* (swordfish), *lüfer* (blue-fish),

Fish is cooked before it is even landed at the quayside in Istanbul

kalkan (turbot) and *levrek* (bass) are among the most tasty.

The best known *meze* or hors d'œuvres are *dolma*, vegetables such as peppers, aubergines, vine leaves and cabbage leaves stuffed with rice, pine nuts and currants. *Zeytinyağlılar*, dishes of cold vegetables in olive oil, include *imam bayıldı*, meaning 'the priest fainted', a dish of aubergines stuffed with fried tomatoes, onions and garlic. *Böreks* are delicious small pies of filo or flaky pastry filled with meat or cheese.

Desserts are usually based on milk, such as *sütlaç* (cold rice pudding), or pastries soaked in syrup, like *baklava* (flaky pastry stuffed with nuts in syrup) and *tel kadayıf*, shredded wheat with

nuts and syrup. And if other sweet goodies such as *hanim göbegi* (lady's navel), *dilber dudagi* (lips of a beauty), or *lokum* (Turkish delight) do not tempt, there are fresh grapes, peaches, apricots, figs or a slice of melon to finish your meal.

At street corners you will encounter Turkish youths selling circular bread rolls called *simit*; sandwich salesmen making up their products on the spot; and other vendors selling corn-on-the-cob and a great variety of Turkish pastries.

Among alcoholic drinks are the light Turkish beer, excellent red and white wines and the national drink *raki*, which clouds when water is added, giving it the name 'lion's milk'.

Popular non-alcoholic drinks include *ayran*, a mixture of yoghurt, water and a pinch of salt, fresh fruit juices and strong Turkish coffee.

SHOPPING

Virtually every city, town and holiday resort in Turkey offers a good range of shops, from modern stores and boutiques to bustling bazaars and markets brimming with Turkish crafts, where bargaining is the order of the day. Copper and brassware, *meerschaum* ('white gold') pipes, alabaster and onyx ware all make good souvenirs; porcelain goods and hand-painted ceramics are also good value, with beautifully decorated plates and ornamental tiles in all sizes. But perhaps the intricately-patterned carpets are the most evocative mementoes. Leather goods, especially coats and jackets, are inexpensive, although of wildly varying quality,

and light cotton fabrics fashioned into stylish European designs are another good buy. Especially popular are tee-shirts imitating designer labels.

Gold and silver jewellery is often sold by weight rather than design with lots to choose from.

ACCOMMODATION

Tourism is fairly new to Turkey and consequently, although the building of hotels, holiday villages and self-catering apartments is proceeding apace, much of the existing accommodation is not of the same standard that visitors may have become used to. Generally speaking, older hotels and *pensions (pansiyons)* will typically have traditional-style heavy furniture, no shower tray in some of the bathrooms – just a hole in the floor – and be fairly spartan if not extremely basic. Nor are beds always interior sprung divans; they may be built-in platform beds or a mattress on a wire base.

● **Local tourism bureaux** can provide information and make reservations (see under individual cities/towns/sites for addresses and telephone numbers).

NIGHTLIFE

Turkey is not noted for its pulsating nightlife, but the growth in tourism in recent years has seen discos opening up in many of the major holiday resorts, and a proliferation of 'folklore' evenings complete with belly dancing. Istanbul and Ankara both offer a good selection of nightclubs serving excellent food accompanied by varied entertainment. Otherwise, night-time activities tend to centre on *al fresco* dining, perhaps accompanied by Turkish music.

HOW TO BE A LOCAL

If you want to be a local you need to know what is going on, and for this the *Turkish Daily News*, the leading English-language newspaper, is to be recommended. Hospitality is important to the Turkish people and should not be refused, or abused. Turks appreciate sincerity and are adept at discerning falseness. The normal form of greeting is to shake hands. Visitors should always respect Islamic customs if they do not wish to offend. Informal wear is acceptable, but scanty beachwear should be confined to the beach or poolside. It is courteous during the time of Ramazan, to refrain from drinking alcohol and, in the eastern part of the country, not to eat or drink in public. Smoking is widely accepted, but it is prohibited in cinemas, theatres, city buses and shared taxis (*dolmus*). When visiting mosques be sure to enter in stockinged feet or wear the felt overshoes provided. To be truly accepted as a local, you must be able to bargain well. Bargaining is a game enjoyed by the Turks and no-one will be offended if there is no deal at the end.

TIGHT BUDGET

Holidaymakers on a tight budget can enjoy the attractions of Turkey if they plan carefully.

● Flight-only charter flights are considerably cheaper than scheduled flights. The cost of scheduled flights can be reduced

Part of the annual festival in Ephesus takes place in the ancient Grand Theatre, which once seated 25,000

if you book some time in advance.

● Package holidays are cheaper in April, May, June and October.

● Inexpensive small hotels, pensions (*pansiyons*) and village rooms can be found everywhere.

● Avoid well-developed resorts and venture off the beaten track.

● Seek out places where the locals eat, rather than the 'touristy' restaurants.

● Rail transport is among the cheapest available.

● Shop for souvenirs in markets and bazaars – and remember to bargain well.

FESTIVALS, FAIRS AND SPECIAL EVENTS

January
Camel Wrestling Festival, Selçuk
April–May
International Arts Festival, Ankara
Ephesus International Festival of Culture and Tourism
May
International Music and Folklore Festival, Silifke
June
Atatürk Culture Festival, Aksaray
Marmaris Festival
Bergama Festival
Çesme Sea and Music Festival
Ihlara Tourism and Art Week, Amasya
June–July
Istanbul International Art and Culture Festival
Grease Wrestling, Edirne
July
International Culture and Art Festival, Bursa
International Folk Dance Festival, Samsun
Ceramic Festival, Kütahya
August
Troy Festival, Çanakkale

August–September
Izmir International Fair
September
Mersin Art and Culture Festival
October
International Mediterranean Song Contest, Antalya
December
International St Nicholas Symposium, Demre
Mevlana Commemoration Ceremony, Konya

CLIMATE
Turkey is a vast country, and climatic conditions vary enormously. The Mediterranean and Aegean coasts enjoy the most agreeable year-round weather, but visitors should be prepared for extreme heat in the height of the summer, and not over-do the sunbathing in the early stages. The Mediterranean tends to be even hotter and more humid than the Aegean. The Black Sea region is cooler, and rainier, while visits to eastern Turkey are not recommended in winter due to the extreme cold.

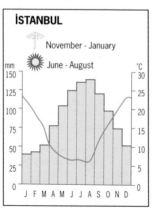

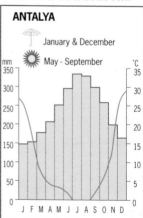

DIRECTORY

Arriving

Entry Formalities

Nationals of the United Kingdom or Eire require a visa to enter Turkey, available at border gates or ports of entry and valid for three months. For longer stays, visas must be obtained from the nearest Turkish Embassy or Consulate. For nationals of other EC countries (except Italy), the United States, Canada, Australia and New Zealand, a valid passport will suffice.

By Air

Many international airlines operate direct scheduled services to Istanbul and Ankara, from where there are frequent connections to Turkey's main holiday centres. An increasing number of charter flights are being operated to Turkey, especially to Izmir, Antalya, Adana and Dalaman, serving the Aegean and Mediterranean holiday resorts.

By Sea

Several foreign shipping companies have regular passenger services to the ports of Istanbul, Izmir, Kusadası, Bodrum, Marmaris, Alanya and Antalya.

● **Car Ferries:** Turkish Maritime Lines sails regularly from April to November. The Venice–Izmir–Antalya service sails weekly from April to November. In addition there are services to North Cyprus: the Mersin (Içel)–Magosa line runs three times a week all year.

There are also summer services to North Cyprus from Tasucu, near Silifke (daily except Sunday), and from Alanya to Girne (weekly).

Popular Ölü Deniz Bay has a spectacular backdrop

DIRECTORY

You may not have seen before a baker's boy like this one selling his wares outside a Konya mosque

By Rail
There are regular train services to Istanbul from principal European cities and an efficient rail network connects most major Turkish cities.

By Road
Driving to Turkey from most European countries is a lengthy and daunting undertaking, for instance, London to Istanbul is approximately 1,865 miles (3,000km). All principal routes meet at Belgrade for an onward journey via Nis, Sofia, Edirne and Istanbul. To reach Belgrade from the north, travel via Nuremberg, Linz, Vienna and Budapest, or Stuttgart, Munich, Salzburg, Ljubljana and Zagreb; from the south, via Geneva, Venice and Ljubljana. Seek advice first about the safety of driving in what was once Yugoslavia. Car ferries from Venice provide a useful short cut, see **Car Ferries** (page 113).

Baths
Because of the emphasis placed on cleanliness by Islam, there have been public baths (*hamam*) in Turkey since medieval times and many of those in use today are in fine buildings. There are separate baths for men and women, or separate days when they can use them. Bathers leave their clothes in a cubicle and proceed, wrapped in a towel (*pestemal*), to be rubbed down by a bath attendant on a large heated stone (*gobek tasi*). If the heat proves too much, you can lie for a while in a cooler room.

Camping
Ministry of Tourism approved campsites are still few, but are situated in the main tourist centres and are generally open from April or May to October. The 'Mocamp Kervansaray' chain of sites is recommended. Camping outside official sites is possible but not advisable.

Chemist – see Health

Crime
The one cardinal rule, of course, is not to import or use drugs in Turkey. Though pick-pocketing, bag-snatching and mugging are practically unheard of in Turkey, it is still sensible not to carry all your valuables and travel documents while sightseeing.

Customs Regulations
Foreign tourists may take into Turkey duty-free: personal effects; medical items; one still and one video camera, with up to 5 rolls of film each; 200 cigarettes and 50 cigars or 200g tobacco (an additional 400 cigarettes, 100 cigars and 500g of tobacco may

be imported if purchased at the Turkish duty-free shops on arrival); 1.5kg coffee; 1kg sweets and 1kg chocolate; 5 (100cc) or 7 (70cc) bottles of alcohol; 5 bottles (maximum size 120ml each) of perfume; and gifts not exceeding 500 Deutschmarks in value. Valuable items should be registered in the owner's passport for control on exit. The bringing into the country or use of narcotics is strictly forbidden and subject to heavy penalties. On exit, the export of antiquities is forbidden. For currency restrictions see **Money Matters**.

Domestic Travel

Air

Turkish Airlines and Istanbul Airlines provide a network of flights from the international airports of Istanbul, Ankara, Izmir, Trabzon, Dalaman, Antalya and Adana to major Turkish cities.

Sea

Turkish Maritime Lines operates year-round passenger and car ferry services from Istanbul to Izmir and to ports on the Mediterranean coast, and the Black Sea Line to Samsun, Rize, Trabzon (and ports between).

Rail

Rail services connect major cities, with an express service between Istanbul, Ankara and Izmir, but it is usually a lot quicker by bus. Trains have sleeping cars, couchettes and restaurant cars, offering first and second class service. In Istanbul eastbound trains leave from Haydarpasa Station on the Asian side.

Buses

There is an extensive network of inexpensive services which run day and night between all Turkish cities. Services are frequent, though on many routes there is no set timetable. Coaches depart from the bus station (*otogar*) in large towns and from the centre of town in smaller places.

Taxis

Taxis are numerous in all Turkish cities and are recognisable by their yellow colour and illuminated 'taxi' signs. The fare shown on the meter is according to kilometres travelled. The *dolmus* (marked with a yellow band) is a shared taxi which follows specific routes and is much cheaper than a taxi.

Driving

Cars

Cars, minibuses caravans, towed sea craft and motorcycles can be taken into Turkey for up to three months without a Carnet de Passage or triptique. The vehicle is simply registered in the owner's passport and this registration is cancelled when the owner leaves the country. For longer stays, apply to the Turkish Touring and Automobile Association for a triptique; otherwise the vehicle must leave and re-enter the country after three months. If you wish to visit another country from Turkey without your car, you should take the vehicle to the nearest Customs Office (*Gümrük Müdürlügü*) so that the registration of the car in your passport can be cancelled.

DIRECTORY

• **Traffic circulation**: Traffic circulates on the right and traffic on the right should be given way to. The Turkish Highway Code is similar to those of European countries. Outside the cities, traffic moves comparatively freely, the exception being the Istanbul–Ankara highway. There is a 31mph (50kph) speed limit in urban centres, a 55mph (90kph) limit outside urban centres and a 74mph (120kph) limit on express motorways.

• **Petrol**: Petrol prices are generally below most European ones, though there are slight variations. The brands of petrol available are: Petrol Ofisi, Turk Petrol, BP, Mobil and Shell. 'Super' (4 star), 'Normal' (2 star), and lead-free (*kursunsuz*) petrol can be found all over the country except in the most isolated parts. Filling stations are well distributed and those on the main highways often have service stations and restaurants attached, and are usually open 24 hours.

• **Road signs**: Turkish road signs conform to the International Protocol on Road Signs. Archaeological and historical sites have yellow signposts.

• **Insurance**: Motorists should have either:-
a) Green Card international insurance endorsed for Turkish territory, both Europe and Asia, or;
b) Turkish third party insurance, which can be obtained from any of the insurance agencies at the frontier posts.

• **Driving licence**: A national licence is acceptable, though an international licence could be useful.

A million or so Turks are still nomadic, especially in summer; these nomads have camped in the mountains by Lake Van in eastern Turkey near the Iranian border

Car Breakdown – Accidents and Repairs

In the case of an accident, a report is essential and the police must be notified. If you hold a motoring club credit cheque, the Turkish motoring club, Turkiye Turing ve Otomobil Kurumu (TTOK) will carry out necessary repairs and forward the bill in Swiss Francs. If you possess an AIT or FIA assistance booklet, the TTOK will bear the cost of transporting your damaged vehicle, via Customs, to your home. If you have to leave the vehicle in Turkey for later collection, it must be taken to a Customs Office (*Gümrük Müdürlügü*) so that its endorsement on your passport

head office (tel: (1) 2314631);
Edirne – frontier office (tel: (1818)
1034, 1327); Ankara (tel: (4)
4317648-9); Izmir (tel: (51)
217149, 226387); Bolu (tel: (461)
12528-9), open 08.30–17.00 hrs.

Car Hire

Car hire in Turkey is not cheap,
and many of the vehicles offered
for rent are of dubious standard.
Best bets are probably Hertz,
Avis, Budget and Europcar which
are extending their outlets to
embrace most of the principal
airports, cities and holiday
resorts. It is important, also, to
consider that the final cost may
be higher than originally
estimated, since a 10 per cent tax
is added to the bill. Minimum age
to hire a car is 21. You will need
your driving licence (held for at
least a year) and an international
licence could be useful.

Electricity

The standard voltage in Turkey is
220 volts AC, and the sockets are
of the two-pronged, round-pin
variety, so adaptors (also for US
visitors – a voltage transformer)
will be necessary if you want
to use a hairdryer or electric
razor, etc.

Embassies and Consulates

Britain: Embassy – Sehit Ersan
Caddesi 46A, Çankaya, Ankara
(tel: (4) 4274310-5); Consulate –
Mesrutiyet Caddesi 34, Tepebası,
Beyoglu, Istanbul (tel: (1)
2447540).
Ireland: Consulate – Cumhuriyet
Caddesi 26A, Elmadag, Istanbul
(tel: (1) 2466025).
United States: Embassy – Atatürk
Bulvarı 110, Kavaklidere, Ankara
(tel: (4) 4265470); Consulate –

can be deleted. Without this, you
cannot leave the country. Make
Customs aware that the vehicle
will be collected at some point –
otherwise it may be considered
abandoned after three months. If
your vehicle is totally wrecked
and has to be abandoned, it must
also be transported to a Customs
Office for cancellation of your
passport endorsement. If your
vehicle is stolen you must obtain
a certificate from the governor of
the province (*Vali*), again so that
your passport endorsement can
be cancelled before you leave
the country.

● **Repairs:** There are numerous
repair garages in towns (usually
grouped along special streets)
and along principal highways.
Spare parts for the most common
makes of cars are usually fairly
easily available.

In addition, assistance can be
sought from Turkiye Turing ve
Otomobil Kurumu: Istanbul –

DIRECTORY

Mesrutiyet Caddesi 104–8,
Tepebası, Beyoglu, Istanbul (tel:
(1) 2513602).
Canada: Embassy – Nenehatun
Caddesi 75, Gaziosmanpasa,
Ankara (tel: (4) 4361275-9).
Australia: Embassy – Nenehatun
Caddesi 83, Gaziosmanpasa,
Ankara (tel: (4) 4361240-5).

Emergency Telephone Numbers
Police: 055
Fire: 000
Ambulance: 077

Health Regulations
No vaccinations are normally
required by the Turkish
authorities, though there is a risk
of malaria in the Çukurova/
Amikova area from March to
November and in southeast
Anatolia from mid-May to mid-
October. It is advisable to take
out medical insurance and
ensure that, if you intend visiting
both the European and Asian
sections of Turkey, the policy
covers both areas.
Visitors unaccustomed to foreign
food can sometimes experience
stomach upsets, so it is useful to
take appropriate medication with
you. Alternatively, this can be
obtained from Turkish chemist
shops (*eczane*) which stock a
good range of medications to
cure most ailments.
Tap water is generally safe, but
bottled water is cheap and always
a wiser option. In emergencies,
dial 077 for an ambulance, or
contact the American Hospital in
Istanbul, Güzelbahçe Sokagi 20,
Nisantası (tel: (1) 2314050), or
the American Hospital in Ankara,
Balgat Amerikan Tesisleri (tel:
(4) 4259945).

Holidays
Public:

1 January	New Year's Day
23 April	National Independence and Children's Day
19 May	Atatürk Commemoration and Youth and Sports Day
30 August	Victory Day
29 October	Republic Day (previous day is half day holiday)

Religious:
There are two religious holidays
celebrated in Turkey. The first is
the 3½ day 'Seker Bayramı'
(Sugar Festival), when sweets are
eaten to mark the end of the fast
of Ramazan. The second is the 4½
day 'Kurban Bayramı' (Festival of
Sacrifice), when sacrificial sheep
are slaughtered and their meat
distributed to the poor. The dates
of these festivals change
according to the Moslem
calendar. During public and
religious holidays shops and
government offices are closed.

Lost Property
Reports of lost or stolen property
should be made to the local
tourism police.

Media
Newspaper: The main English
language daily is the *Turkish
Daily News.*
Radio: The 'Voice of Turkiye'
(VOT-TRT) broadcasts in English
as the principal foreign language,
with news, music and some
practical information for foreign
visitors. Frequencies include:-
Mhz
101.9 – – Istanbul, Kusadası,
Nevsehir;
100.5 – Izmir;

97.4 – Bodrum;
101.6 – Çesme;
103.0 – Marmaris;
100.6 – Antalya;
101.0 – Pamukkale.
Television: Channels 2 and 5 give the news in English each night after the 22.00hrs Turkish news.

Money Matters
The monetary system is the Turkish Lira (TL). Coins in circulation are of 50, 100, 500, 1,000 and 2,500 lira, and banknotes in denominations of 1,000, 5,000, 10,000, 20,000, 50,000, 100,000 and 250,000 lira. There is no restriction on the amount of foreign or local currency that can be taken into Turkey, but should be declared on arrival to avoid difficulty on departure. Up to the equivalent of US$5,000 in foreign or local currency may be exported.
Exchange slips: Currency exchange receipts should be kept for re-converting Turkish lira (up to the equivalent of US$100) into foreign currency on departure, and also as proof that any large purchase, such as a carpet, has been bought with legally exchanged foreign currency.
Banks: See below for opening times.
Credit cards: Most international credit cards are becoming more widely accepted in the larger cities and resorts, but do not depend on them. They are unlikely to be accepted in smaller restaurants or villages, for instance, so it is advisable to take travellers' cheques, Eurocheques or foreign currency which can be easily cashed at any bank.

An enterprising shoe-shine man and his attractive stall in Istanbul

Opening Times
Banks: Monday to Friday 08.30–12.00hrs and 13.30–17.00hrs.
Government offices: Monday to Friday 08.30–12.30hrs and 13.30–17.30hrs.
Post offices: Major post offices are open 08.00–20.00hrs Monday to Saturday and 09.00–19.00hrs Sunday, though international telephone offices attached are open until 24.00hrs; smaller post offices are open as Government offices (see above).
Shops: 09.30–13.00hrs and 14.00–19.00hrs. Closed Sundays. Covered Bazaar, Istanbul 08.00–19.00hrs. Closed Sundays.
Museums: Most Turkish museums are open daily, except Mondays, but it would be wise to check first. Palaces are open every day except on Mondays and Thursdays. The Topkapı Palace in Istanbul is closed on Tuesdays.

DIRECTORY

Ancient and modern – olives and communications spheres at Mardin

Personal Safety

Apart from the possibility of stomach upsets brought on by eating unfamiliar food, there is not much to worry about when travelling in Turkey. Mosquitoes can be a nuisance – it is wise to take repellents with you because they are not easily obtainable on the spot – and you should be wary of snakes, some poisonous, when scrambling among unexcavated ruins. (See also **Crime**).

Pharmacist – see Health

Police

In rural areas, law and order are upheld not by the police – who operate in plain clothes – but by armed and uniformed members of the *jandarma*, a section of the army. Although a disconcerting sight to first-time visitors, they do keep trouble to a minimum. Police operate as usual in towns. There are also tourism police (see **Lost Property**).

Post Office

Turkish post offices are easily recognisable by their yellow 'PTT' signs. Letterboxes are yellow and set in walls, though they can be hard to find.
Should you wish to have mail sent to you, it should be addressed: Posterestant, Merkez Postanesi, and the town. (See also **Opening Times – Post offices**).

Student and Youth Travel

All young people and students travelling through the member organisations of BITS, FIYTO, and ISTC, and holding ISIC, INTERAIL, BIGE and YIEE cards of these organisations, can make use of some of the excellent hostels and centres located in various parts of Turkey. For further information contact: Yüsek Ögrenim Kredi ve Yurtlar Kurumu Genel Müdürlügü, Kıbrıs Caddesi 4, Kurtulus/Ankara (tel: (4) 4319575 and 4311100).

Student reductions: Many travel operators recognise the ISTC card and accordingly grant reductions to holders. Turkish Airlines give a 00 per cent discount, Turkish State Railways a 30 per cent discount, Turkish Maritime Lines 00 per cent, and many long-distance coaches up to 50 per cent off fares. In addition, museums, cinemas and concert halls allow a 50 per cent reduction. FIYTO card holders are admitted free to museums and sites.

Telephones

For local, inter-city and international calls, tokens – *jetons* – are required, obtainable from post offices. Phone cards are also available. To make an international call, first dial 9 then, after a new tone, 9 again. Then dial the country code (Britain 44; Ireland 353; USA and Canada 1; Australia 63; New Zealand 64), the local code – minus the initial '0' – then the number. For the international operator dial 528–23–03.

Time

Local time is 2 hours ahead of GMT; 7 hours ahead of US Eastern Standard Time; 8 hours behind Australia; and 10 hours behind New Zealand. Daylight saving (GMT+3) operates between late March and late September, so from late September to late October Turkey is only 1 hour ahead of Britain.

Tipping

A service charge is automatically added to most bills, but it is nevertheless customary to leave a little extra. Where a service charge is not included, as in some smaller restaurants, a tip of about 10 per cent is usual for friendly and efficient service. It is not necessary to tip drivers of *dolmus* taxis, but with conventional taxis it is customary to round up the fare to the nearest 1,000 lira.

Toilets

Toilets (*tuvalet*) invariably fall well short of the standards to which most holiday-makers are accustomed. Basically, the sewage outlet system outside Turkey's bigger cities simply cannot cope with quantities of toilet paper; as a result, small bins are provided for used paper – not a practice that is particularly appealing, especially when the bins are left unemptied for a few days, as can be the case at some of the smaller hotels and *pensions*. But you are advised to conform, as blocked toilets are just as uninviting. However, the plumbing of smarter hotels in cities is able to deal with toilet paper.

Tourist Offices

(For offices in Turkey, see **Tourism Bureau** under individual cities/towns/sites).

Turkish Information Offices abroad **Britain**: First Floor, 170–173 Piccadilly, London W1V 9DD (tel: (071) 734 8681).

United States: 821 United Nations Plaza, New York, N.Y. 10017 (tel: (212) 986 5050; and 1717 Massachusetts Avenue N.W., Suite 306, Washington D.C. 20036 (tel: (202) 429 9844).

LANGUAGE

Turkish is not an easy language to learn or understand, but although many Turkish people, especialy the younger generation, can speak a smattering of many European languages, knowing a few words and phrases of Turkish will help. The Turkish alphabet is very similar to the Latin alphabet except for a few letters which have special pronunciation:

C	=	j as in *Cami* (mosque), pronounced Jami
ç	=	ch as in *Foça*, pronounced Focha
g	=	unpronounced but serves to extend the preceding vowel, so that *dag* is pronounced Daa
ö	=	oe as in *Göreme*, pronounced Goereme
s	=	sh as in *Kusadası*, pronounced Kushadaseu
ü	=	like the French 'tu', as in *Ürgüp*
ı	=	(undotted 'i') pronounced like the 'a' in the English word 'serial'

The uniforms of these Sultan guards have not changed in design since the 19th century

Everyday Phrases

hello *merhaba*
goodbye *allahaısmarladık* (said by the person leaving)
güle güle (said by the person seeing his or her friend off)
good morning *günaydın*
good evening *iyi aksamlar*
goodnight *iyi geceler*
please *lütfen*
thank you *tesekkür ederim*, or *mersi*
yes *evet*
no *hayır*
there is *var*
there is not *yok*
how are you? *nasılsınız?*
I am well, thank you *iyiyim, tesekkür ederim*

Numbers

1	*bir*	40	*kırk*
2	*iki*	50	*elli*
3	*üç*	60	*altmis*
4	*dört*	70	*yetmis*
5	*bes*	80	*seksen*
6	*altı*	90	*doksan*
7	*yedi*	100	*yüz*
8	*sekiz*	101	*yüzbir*
9	*dokuz*	200	*ikiyüz*
10	*on*	300	*üç yüz*
11	*onbir*	1000	*bin*
20	*yirmi*	2000	*ikibin*
30	*otuz*		

The Time and the Days

when? *ne zaman?*
yesterday *dün*
today *bugün*
tomorrow *yarın*
morning *sabah*
afternoon *ögleden sonra*
evening *aksam*
night *gece*
one hour *bir saat*
what is the time? *saat kaç?*
at what time? *saat kaçta?*
Sunday *Pazar*
Monday *Pazartesi*
Tuesday *Salı*
Wednesday *Çarsamba*
Thursday *Persembe*
Friday *Cuma*
Saturday *Cumartesi*

While Travelling

airport *hava alanı*
port *liman*
town centre *sehir merkezi*
where is it? *nerede?*
is it far? *uzak mı?*
tourism bureau *turizm bürosu*
repair garage *bir tamirci*
a good hotel *iyi bir otel*
a restaurant *bir lokanta*

In the Hotel

a room *bir oda*
two people *iki kisi*
a room with a bathroom *banyolu bir oda*
what is the price? *fiatı nedir?*
hot water *sıcak su*
extra bed *ilave bir yatak*
breakfast *kahvaltı*
butter *tereyag*
coffee *kahve*
tea *çay*
milk *süt*
sugar *seker*
the bill *hesap*

Shopping

gold *altın*
silver *gümüs*
leather *deri*
copper *bakır*
how much is it? *bu ne kadar?*

In the Restaurant

bread *ekmek*
water *su*
mineral water *maden suyu*
fruit juice *meyva suyu*
wine *sarap*
beer *bira*
ice *buz*
meat *et*

LANGUAGE

Refreshing çay, *Turkish tea*

mutton *koyun eti*
lamb *kuzu eti*
beef *sigir eti*
veal *dana eti*
chicken *piliç/tavuk*
fish *balık*

Hors d'œuvre *(mezeler)*
arnavut cigeri spicy fried liver
  with onions
çerkes tavugu cold chicken in
  walnut purée with garlic
çig köfte spicy raw meatballs
tarama fish-roe salad
yaprak dolması stuffed vine
  leaves

Soups *(çorbalar)*
yayla çorbası yoghurt soup
dügün çorbası meat soup with egg
  yolks
iskembe çorbası tripe soup

Grills *(izgaralar)*
bonfile fillet steak
döner kebap lamb grilled on a
  revolving spit
pirzola lamb chops
sis kebap grilled lamb on
  skewers
sis köfte grilled meatballs

Pilafs *(pilav)*
sade pilav plain rice pilaf

iç pilav rice with pine nuts,
currants and onions
bulgur pilavı cracked wheat pilaf

Cold vegetables in olive oil
(zeytinyaglılar)
imam bayıldı split aubergine with
  tomatoes and onions
kabak kızartması fried baby
  marrow served with yoghurt
patlıcan kızartması fried aubergine
  slices with yoghurt
zeytinyaglı fasulye green beans
  in tomato sauce

Savoury pastries *(börekler)*
sigara böregi fried filo pastry
  filled with cheese
su böregi layers of filo pastry
  filled with cheese or meat
talas böregi puff-pastry filled
  with meat

Salads *(salatalar)*
cacık chopped cucumber in
  garlic-flavoured yoghurt
çoban salatası mixed tomato,
  pepper, cucumber and onion
  salad
patlıcan salatası puréed aubergine
  salad
piyaz haricot bean salad

Desserts *(tatlılar)*
baklava flaky-pastry stuffed
  with nuts in syrup
tel kadayıf shredded-wheat
  stuffed with nuts and syrup
sütlaç cold rice pudding
komposto cold stewed fruit
dondurma ice cream

Fruits *(meyvalar)*
grapes *üzüm*
peaches *seftali*
plums *erik*
apricots *kayısı*
cherries *kiraz*
figs *incir*
yellow melon *kavun*
water melon *karpz*

INDEX

ACKNOWLEDGEMENTS

The Automobile Association would like to thank the following photographers and libraries for their assistance in the compilation of this book:

J ALLAN CASH PHOTOLIBRARY Cover –Blue Mosque Istanbul, 11 Peasants, 13 Temple of Apollo, 22 Bitez, 25 Cesme Harbour, 45 Kalkan, 49 Hatay Museum Mosaic, 65 Mother & Child, 83 Street trader, 87 Green Mosque, 88 Troy, 94/5 Lake Van, 116/7 Nomads, 120 Mardin, 122 Sultan guards, 124 Turkish tea.

MARY EVANS PICTURE LIBRARY 12 Grand Bazaar.

INTERNATIONAL PHOTOBANK 4 Alanya, 20 Souvenirs, 59 Side, 80 Rumeli Hisari Castle, 109 Cooking & selling fish.

NATURE PHOTOGRAPHERS LTD 99 Geckos, 105 Painted frog, 107 Butterflies (R Bush), 97 Tree, 104 Turkish farm (N A Callow), 100 Red-footed falcon, 103 Woodpecker (C H Gomersall), 102 Brown Bear (W S Paton), 108 Turtle (J Sutherland), 98 Slender billed gulls (R Tidman).

SPECTRUM COLOUR LIBRARY 7 Pergamon, 17 Bodrum, 18/19 Bodrum Harbour & Castle, 26/7 Lycian cave & tombs, 29 Tombs near Fethiye, 30 Xanthos, 32/3 Izmir Bay, 35 Kusadasi, 36 Ephesus, 39 Marmaris, 41 Pamukkale, 50/1 Antalya, 52 Seljuk bridge, 54 Carpets in Kas, 57 Temple doorway, 61 Cappadocia, 63 Ankara, 66 Urgup, 68 Rock house Goreme, 69 Alaeddin Mosque, 79 Blue Mosque, 89 Sile, 92 Trabzon, 93 Nemrut Dagi, 113 Olu Deniz, 114 Baker's boy, 119 Shoeshine boy.

ZEFA PICTURE LIBRARY (UK) LTD 42/3 Olu Deniz, 71 Across the Bosphorus, 75 Topkapi Palace, 76/7 Sancta Sophia, 85 Grand Bazaar, 111 Grand Theatre.